slightly famous

JAKE SASSEVILLE

City of Sass 1001 Avenue of the Americas Ste 1000 New York, New York 10018 Copyright 2012 by Jake Sasseville All rights reserved, including the right to reproduce this book or portions thereof in any form whatsoever. For interviews or bookings, please call Yvette Noel-Schure at 917-623-8856 or email Carolina@schuremedia.com. Manufactured in the United States of America.

Cover photo by Ka'Lan Jones

Front cover photo edited by : Victoria Ramon

ISBN: 061567013X
ISBN 13: 9780615670133

CITY OF SASS

New York

San Francisco

London

Dedicated to the hard work, long hours, and unapologetic determination of every single person who's ever stood by me even when it wasn't sexy to do so.

Must also appreciate the people who helped me write this tale, including the guy who lived in San Francisco with me for a month helping me organize my thoughts — James McCrae — who is also the editor of this book.

To my best friends Caitlin Engel, Brenton Geiser and Manuel Rappard for helping me realize that this was the book that had to be written, and my long-time friends Bobby Guerette, Adib Birkland and Laura Sturgis for their ideas, guidance and brutal criticism early on.

It takes a village.

Contents

Part One: The Thrill of the Build

How to build a multi-million dollar company in six months

Part Two: The Freedom of the Fall

*Why failing doesn't mean you're a failure, and the anecdotes,
strategies and balls-out approach I used to stage a come back*

Disclaimers

1. This book contains some vulgar language.

2. This book contains some spiritual ideas.

3. We have changed some names to protect the innocent (and the guilty).

Foreword

Many people want to change the world. There are some who actually do. In fairness to everyone else, the world changes due to the sheer momentum of the biological collective. But there are those who, as an individual, cause change. They insist on it. Those individuals affect the masses. It may be a performer, a community leader, or an author. Or it may be a guy from a small town in Maine – a guy who was never meant to be a part of the collective, biological or otherwise.

A Tasmanian devil in Crocs. This is Jake. A tsunami in spanks. This is Jake. If Dame Edna swallowed Martin Short ... again, this is Jake. Jake defies logic to such a degree, and he is a super-cell of emotion, drive, and self-effacing accomplishment. He at once cares deeply about the human condition, yet makes those around him insane with his callous path to achieve a better place for the rest of us.

My first meeting with Jake was in 2004. That afternoon, Starbucks in Columbus Circle (Manhattan, New York) was its usual frenetically charged bee hive of dissonance, driven by countless intertwining and overlapping conversations.

I didn't yet know Jake's voice as we had only communicated via email. Yet his voice was present. He was the voice in the crowd speaking at a different frequency. It didn't matter that he was basically just a kid, 18 years old. His was already the voice of someone who was changing the world – in this case, he was changing mine.

As he spoke to me that day, telling me about his talk show and his plans for success, I remember glancing off over his shoulder out at Central Park across the street. I grew up in New York City and I had been to Central Park a million times. After a while, even the strangers look familiar.

And yet as Jake spoke, everything I knew seemed different. I've never done drugs but from what I know this would be similar to a "high". I understand that there are "good highs" and "bad highs" and knowing Jake for as long as I have, I get it when people have a "bad Jake high."

It wasn't long before I was working with Jake on one of the many iterations of "his show". The show had evolved, migrated and otherwise transmutated itself from talk show to variety show to reality show and back again. It, like its founding father was never really comfortable being categorized. True to form the show I agreed to help produce (and quickly found myself directing) was well, let's just say somewhat *undefined*. However none of that mattered because Jake was "the thing".

Ironic, because Jake was nearly devoid of pop culture knowledge (a critical constant for the host of a talk show). He didn't have very good interview skills. He was unfocused on the present and living in the future (one of his greatest assets I would later figure out).

And yet there is an air of accomplishment that always surrounded him. So while there was no reason in the world that I should have wanted to follow him into Big Bird's nest on the set of Sesame Street (oh yes, he did interview *the* Big Bird), I knew I had to – I knew something special was happening. I knew Jake would find a way. And selfishly, I wanted to be a part of it.

Jake and Big Bird meet on the set of Sesame Street in Queens, New York.

Years later I realized that pretty much everyone puts up with Jake's shenanigans and nonsense because we all want to be a part of something different – something special. And all the crap he puts you through aside, if you are with Jake, you are doing something special. Of course it may also be your epitaph.

Jake allows you to look into him and see yourself in a way you've never experienced. He makes you want to be better while frustrating you beyond words.

But to achieve your "inner Jake", you must let yourself get to know him. And that is something else entirely. It is an invigorating and maddening trek through the land of impossibility.

And when you have reached your Masters class in Jake, it comes down to this. To know Jake you must be willing to let him go. He cannot be contained – not by geographic boundaries, not even by the boundaries of personal relationships. And when he goes, it will always be a shock to your system. Because Jake, like any good drug, is highly addictive and while none of us want to admit it – quite seductive.

Years later – actually only a few months ago as of the writing of this Foreword – Jake called me and said "I'm doing a show, and I want you to direct it." The show of course didn't exist other than in Jake's head, and as he ran through possible scenes of a show based on his life, embracing his "Delusions of Grandeur," I realized the high was back. This one was going to be a good high.

This show was going to be different. This show was the show in my mind's eye I saw Jake doing nearly a decade ago. After his life was deconstructed and reconstituted, *Delusions of Grandeur* was in fact the Jake puree, the essence of Jake, the Jake perfume.

Were it not playing off another popular show or film, I would have suggested we call this one *Jake's Anatomy* or *Being Jake Sasseville*. But in hindsight, this show couldn't have been called anything else. Because to get where he is and where only he can go, it requires the deft craftsmanship of a consistent stream of *Delusions of Grandeur*.

As I was sitting in my backyard, basking in the Arizona sunshine, listening to Jake talk about this new show, an old friend was back. The high was taking over. And like many illicit substances, this one too will come calling for you. It will knock you on your ass, only then to reach out its hand to help you back up. This drug has a street name. It's called Jake.

David Sonkin, DGA 2004-2010
Executive Producer/Director, *The Edge with Jake Sasseville,* 2004-2006
Co-executive producer/Director, *Delusions of Grandeur,* 2012

Introduction

I have heard it said that the first ingredient of success – the earliest spark in the dreaming youth – is this; dream a great dream.

— JOHN APPLEMAN

Growing up in Maine

The year is 2002 and I'm a sophomore at Edward Little High School in Auburn, Maine. I've grown up only in Maine so far, the whitest state in the nation. I'm in Honors English class. Ms. Bilodeau is a 22-year-old hippie who's fresh out of college and obsessed with literature and good writing.

I'm 300 pounds, barely able to fit in the desks that must be older than my parents and barely got into this accelerated English class. I'm the fattest one in class of 400, and I don't really like to read much, either. My flamboyant humor seems to mask the insecurity of being fat *and* not doing my homework.

I'm sweating like a wildebeest despite the sub-zero temperatures on a sunny February day. I'm out of breath of course, because I had to walk up two flights of stairs to English class. I didn't hesitate to stop at the school store and grab Starbursts *and* Skittles for the climb.

My brother Alex, 11, was diagnosed with cancer recently, during my freshman year of high school, but for a few months at least, he seems to be in remission. That'll change soon enough.

When Alex was diagnosed with cancer, by default, I became emancipated. I was 15 years old. My parents lives became about saving my brother's. Left to fend for myself, because my parents knew I could, I moved in with my Aunt Lisa-Marie for a few months.

Back in English class, I cracked a joke as class started. As usual, Ms. Bilodeau had to aggressively silence me. For me, the line between wrecking havoc like a normal teenager and going over the line (and straight to juvenile detention) was a thin one. Story of my life.

I chose to go to a public high school over a private one because if I went to the private one, I'd run the risk of being even more indoctrinated by Catholic theology rather than becoming a well-rounded, worldly citizen accepting of all Religions. Best decision I made.

Also, another benefit to public school: I could shop in the Big and Tall section at J.C. Penny's instead of out of uniform magazine.

The same week Alex was diagnosed with acute myeloid leukemia (the most aggressive type of childhood leukemia), my friend Ezra Horne invited me to be a character on his TV show for local access called *What!?*

I played a news anchor, wore a silk bright green shirt with a polka dot tie. I looked ridiculous, and acted even more so. I loved every minute of it. In a sense, TV for me became an escape to my real world that was crumbling. Not only did I think my piss-poor performance was worthy of applause and ovations, but I thought I could do TV and become quite famous for it.

My delusions started young. Luckily, my will and focus has been stronger than all the naysayers who have rightfully agreed, that I am indeed, delusional. Even luckier for me, my parents opted for intense therapy that sort of worked, and not medication. The therapists wanted me medicated. My parents said NO. Medication would have dulled the brilliance.

Thanks mom and dad.

I just finished reading Mark Mathabane's autobiography, *Kaffir Boy* for my English class. From adolescence to adulthood, *Kaffir Boy* chronicles Mark Mathabane's life in an apartheid-torn South Africa in the 60s and 70s and how he escaped. He made the critical decision to leave his family behind and take advantage of a tennis scholarship at St. Louis University offered by tennis legend Arthur Ashe. He'd later bring his entire family— with the help of Oprah Winfrey—to the United States.

I fell in love with Mark Mathabane's story. It was one of the only books I *actually* read that year in English class. Perhaps it was because of my brother's struggle to survive, my family being ripped at the seams financially to cover medical costs or my own coming of age challenges (being in the closet is comfy – for a while anyway.) Whatever it was, consciously or unconsciously, I knew I had to meet Mark Mathabane.

"I'd like to find a way to have him come to Maine," I announced during a discussion session in Ms. Bilodeau's English class.

The class chuckled. They thought I was nuts.

Ms. Bilodeau redeemed me.

"That'd be great, Jake."

Bilodeau moved on, but I didn't.

In the week that followed, I made several calls to Mathabane's representatives, inquiring about coming to Maine. I brokered deals with his speaking agents in New York City as my voice was still cracking. One of his agents even called me m'am.

I convinced Bates College, a prestigious liberal arts school in my hometown, to pay for a large portion of Mathabane's fee.

One night when I was in my bedroom doing homework, I had the idea to call Maine native Stephen "I fucking wrote *The Stand, Pet Cemetery and Christine*" King for the rest of the money.

I didn't know Stephen at the time, but I thought if I *acted* like I did, that he would give me the money.

To my surprise, instead of getting Stephen, I got Tabitha, his wife. She and their foundation, "The Stephen and Tabitha King Foundation" – somehow, someway – agreed to give me the rest of the money.

I'm a power broker at 16.

Taking a crack at television

I had been thinking about creating *The Edge with Jake Sasseville* ever since my stint on *What!?* With Mark Mathabane coming to town, it seemed like the perfect first show.

I loved television even though I had never done it before. I loved the idea of telling Mark Mathabane's story.

At the television studio that day, I was woefully undereducated and underprepared. Between the tiger-skin background for my backdrop and Neil Diamond's "Coming to America" as my theme song, I was obviously still learning about culture outside of Maine.

I wanted to be famous for more than just being famous. I was deliberate and whimsical in my approach, even in these early days. I was acting on ambition and impulse. It seemed to work. I got rewarded for it.

Moments before Mathabane arrived at the studio, my friends (a teenage TV staff of 6) were in a flurry with last minute preparations for the interview. We were using a local access TV studio owned by the City of Auburn.

An autographed photo we found that Mark Mathabane gave to one of my friends, Renee. Pictured here are my teenage friends and crew of *The Edge* in 2001, from left to right, Amy, Jillian, Renee, Christina, Matt, Bobby and below are Mark Mathabane and me.

I was directing the staff like I was a TV veteran. The problem was none of us had a clue what we were doing. I learned an important lesson that day: act like you know what you're doing, and people will follow.

During the interview, I played many roles: part teenage fan, part Oprah wannabee, and part Maine ambassador. The interview was surprisingly in-depth for a kid who thought a tiger backdrop was appropriate for his distinguished South African guest.

My last question to Mark Mathabane was a simple one.

"What's next for you, Mark?"

His answer was eloquent.

"I will continue sharing my story and my message," Mark said, in his soft voice. "For I know as long as there remains unrest and pain with humanity, as long as I have brothers and sisters suffering, I cannot myself rest."

And what did I do?

I uncontrollably started to weep. When I say weep, I mean full-on ugly cry weep.

It was pitiful and endearing all at once. No one knew what to do. My hormones were fucking out of control.

The show was live and we still had to wrap it up.

The director impulsively started playing "Coming to America." The overture of violins engulfed the studio.

Then the drums.

Cue Neil Diamond.

"Far, we've been traveling far... we found our home."

Nervous laughter rumbled. I was still crying, looking utterly helpless.

"Free, we only want to be free; we huddle close, and hang on to a dream."

I kept hugging Mark like my life depended on it. I counted five hugs in twenty-seconds when I watched the VHS later on. My nose ran all over Mark Mathabane's Armani suit. I didn't want to let go and Mark was too nice to push away.

Awkward turtle moment.

"On the boats and on the plane, they coming to America."

I saw the local news people writing in their notepads. Never one to avoid a headline, I thought all this crying business and embarrassment might actually get me some good press.

It was awfully uncomfortable. But, in some strange way, with no prior television experience and everyone telling me we had done a great thing that day, I recognized the power of television and my place in it. I'm very fortunate that I had a strong idea of what I wanted my life to be about at an early age, and that I had the sheer delusions to pursue it.

(While still in Maine, and still on local access, I started to crawl my way through Hollywood, very much from the outside, eventually landing such "big" interviews with Jim Dougherty, Marilyn Monroe's first husband, Zoe Zanidackis, a CBS Survivor contestant from season three, and eventually, the entire cast of the NBC hit show, *Will and Grace,* all before the ripe age of 18.)

Sean Hayes, who played Jack on NBC's *Will and Grace,* graciously sits through an interview with me when I was 17, despite the fact that I was woefully unprepared, going so far as to cite projects that he did 10 years prior, as if they happened that year.

Fast forward eight years: 2009

I experienced a huge surge of success with *The Edge with Jake Sasseville.* I launched after *Jimmy Kimmel Live* on ABC affiliates the year prior. I built a multi-million dollar production studio and, quite literally, felt what it was like to be famous... for a second. I had publicists and producers, assistants and hair people. Folks recognized me on the street and I was seen at parties with Jerry Seinfeld and the Mayor.

Then, I leapt ungracefully into obscurity for 13-months after I drove my company unintentionally into hundreds of thousands of dollars in debt and faced bankruptcy. I was ripped off the air and my life fell apart.

Over a year later I re-launched *The Edge* in syndication on CW and FOX affiliates, thanks to the money of Denny's, Coke, a couple of smart business maneuvers and a great team.

And now, in October, 2009, I was experiencing another downturn (seems to be a pattern for those who wish to be wildly successful). *The Edge* was on FOX and CW nationwide until 2011. I had a TV show airing repeats with no money to produce more episodes. I was losing my footing (and my mind) and was still feeling the aftershocks of a partial bankruptcy.

Quite frankly, I wasn't sure I wanted to continue pursuing my "dream job" of late-night TV stardom. It all seemed a bit daunting and suddenly wasn't as glamorous or easy as I thought it would be.

I'm not one to whine (I'm far more skilled at denial) so I decided I'd take my friend Adib Birkland up on an offer to go on a road trip and see U2 in concert in Oklahoma City.

Denial is the sweetest thing, especially when you have enablers like amazing friends and ridiculous partnerships with airlines like Air Tran Airways, who had been generously providing free, unlimited, first-class airline tickets anywhere I wanted to fly. (At its peak over a three-year successful trade partnership, I was using $30,000 a month of free airline tickets for friends, family, co-workers and anyone else I decided to fly thanks to Air Tran.)

The "real world" was forcing me to choose between my childhood dreams or to move on to something more "practical." (I've always thought a former megalomaniacal talk show host would make a great child psychologist.)

Adventure to steady the mind.

Adib and I decided we'd fly to Kansas and drive west as long as we could, without missing the U2 show in Oklahoma on Sunday night. We flew into Wichita on Friday, and drove west through Greensburg, a town that had been destroyed by a tornado. We met up with the preacher's wife in the town square, whom I hit on.

There were remnants of a meteorite nearby, and I dropped clues to the same preacher's wife that I might steal it, alarming her, and causing her to phone the local sheriff.

Whoopsies.

Later on the trip, Adib and I were moderately impressed by the world's largest hand-dug well and cows that were making sweet love in the pastures (we even did a u-turn because I missed one particularly entertaining cow fuck).

We drove to New Mexico and found a freaky motel among the neon lights on Route 66, where we were a little concerned that we'd be sexually or physically compromised during our sleep by the man at the front desk.

After driving all the next day, we had a sushi dinner in Colorado Springs (where the wait-staff was afraid of the little Asian woman who ran the joint – she apparently hit them frequently). The next morning we drove to Pike's Peak in Colorado – a breathtaking tourist trap.

Even with the fanfare and laughs, it felt awfully lonely for me. I didn't know where to turn and I didn't know how to save my business.

Adib and me preparing for our road trip. The shirt says: "Ahem, I'm a little (picture of a horse) today." Ironic that we both had on the same attire.

Freedom Fries and Coping Mechanisms

I developed survival techniques when I was younger. At 16 years old, after my brother was re-diagnosed with acute myeloid leukemia (AML) for the second time, a year after he was declared in remission, I did what any good brother and son would do – I checked out of my public high school and left for a junior year high school exchange program in France (my brother gave me his blessing long before I applied).

When I arrived in Pontivy, France in November 2003 after three rejected student visa applications (I'm also persistent as hell), my first host family was abusive and the organization refused to transfer me. The abuse was minor. Some verbal tango in a language I didn't speak and generally ignoring me when I asked for help with translations.

However, at one particularly memorable event at the dinner table, the host father stood up, grabbed the mother's head by her hair as she ate, cocked it back, grabbed the bread knife, and pretended to saw her fucking neck off.

Their three biological kids laughed. Normal behavior is all relative, I supposed. When I saw this simulated slaughtering of a human being at the dinner table, I choked on my supper – cow tongue and pig brain. I left the house immediately, locked myself in a hotel in another town and refused to come out until I was transferred.

I was re-assigned to another school in another part of France and I was on the move for the second time in as many months. I was a junior in high school and back home at Boston Children's Hospital my brother was receiving a bone marrow transparent and his recovery was unfavorable. While horrific looking back, it taught me how to cope.

Revelations in the mountains

Adib and I got separated roughly four hours into our hike. I appreciated the time on my own.

I found a landing with some grass that overlooked the mountains. It was a brisk fall afternoon.

I gazed upward to the sky, feeling totally lost and directionless. I thought about jumping, but it was more a curiosity than a desire. I quickly changed my thoughts and considered giving up my so-called "career in television."

Maybe it's just not meant to be.

Then I thought about the goal I set two years before—***win at any cost.***

I decided that whole "at any cost" business was ruining my fucking life. I lost good friendships, ruined my financial success and turned into a madman on an unclear mission.

In some weird way, my moment with Mark Mathabane as a 16-year-old high school sophomore and that day on the mountain in Colorado Springs as a 23-year-old college dropout, merged.

I recognized my passion for contributing massively to people's lives through television. Inspiration and courage comes in the quietest moments when you let yourself go. Trust your intuition rather than your intellect.

This book is the first time I share, as truthfully and honestly as I can, the high highs and low lows of what happens when you pursue your dreams at all costs. It's what happens when you vow to live out loud and share your light so that others can see it, recognize it for themselves, and share their own light with the world.

It's not risky business, but it feels like it at first.

What to expect

Enclosed are a series of truly unbelievable stories – events that you read and you consider their improbability – because they are *that* far off the scale of what is "normal." We all share time together in a society that somehow encourages us to live in the status quo. What happens when you don't? The book is filled with those ideas.

"I've failed over and over and over again in my life and that is why I succeed."

MICHAEL JORDAN

The chance to succeed is simply more thrilling than the inevitably of failure. So why play a small game?

On Monday morning, four days after Adib and I picked up the car in Kansas and paid $8 a day for it, we returned the car to Wichita with a full tank of gas and 1,750 fresh miles added to the odometer.

Enjoy these stories. And, if you find any part of this useful, tell someone about it. Even better, buy them a copy.

PART ONE
THE THRILL OF THE BUILD

How to build a multi-million company in
six months

1

ROCK BANDS, POWER, MONEY AND MOUNTAINTOPS

How I learned the importance of cultivating a belief system that kicks ass

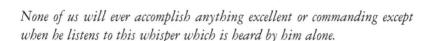

None of us will ever accomplish anything excellent or commanding except when he listens to this whisper which is heard by him alone.

— Ralph Waldo Emerson

It was winter. The year was 2006.

New York is one of those magical cities where chance meetings lead to new friends who change your life forever. It's one of the reasons I moved here, and even when I moved away, I always come back.

"Jakey," my Irish-American friend Paul Romp said to me at a friend's dinner party. "I've talked about you to my friend Mo, and he'd really like to meet you. He's from Europe but is attending film school in New York. I think you guys would get on so well."

"Sure," I replied. "What's his story?"

"Well, he's a filmmaker, and he's a really positive guy. And I think his mom works for some big rock band."

"'Nuff said," I thought.

I've dreamed of money, power and fame since childhood. My dad had my brother and I do a "vision board" each New Year's Eve, and every year I'd have a big dollar sign in the middle of it.

"I'm available Friday afternoon, let's meet at the Whole Foods in Union Square," I confirmed with Paul.

I headed for Whole Foods on Friday afternoon.

I saw a short kid with bleached-blond hair. He had beady eyes, a long black coat and resembled an Irish leprechaun. I assumed it was Mo.

"Hiya," I yelled from afar. "I'm Jake. What's going on, chap?"

Mo looked confused. I think he was stunned that I was so aggressive and forward. Still, he gave me a hug.

Sweet guy.

He spoke fast. He steered the conversation to be about himself. It was like looking into a mirror. I barely kept up. His energy was intense and filled with bursts and spasms.

Mo was awkward, but it drew me in. He suggested that we head for a cup of coffee at a place around the corner. The coffee shop was called "Mo."

He spoke fast. He talked big. He was a great storyteller. I started to probe about his family ties to 'the biggest rock group in the world'. I wasn't great at being discreet, but Mo didn't seem to care. He answered willingly.

"My mom and dad have been working with them for many years," Mo admitted, looking away. "They manage the details of the band's bassist."

I was unapologetic (at least in my mind) about wanting to be in Mo's circle. I wanted to have his access and learn everything about his life. It was the epitome of living vicariously through someone else, but I didn't give a shit. It thrilled me.

I found out that before working for the band, Mo's family, his mom Carrie and his dad Jasper and his sister, came from a modest background. They owned a restaurant in the United Kingdom, and had moved the family to the Isla La Tortuga, a tiny island in the Caribbean, in 1991.

When Mo was six-years-old, all four members of the rock band from Ireland chose their Caribbean getaway as a place of rest before their world tour. The band had just wrapped production on what would become their most critically acclaimed album to date.

The band ended up falling in love with Mo's parents. The bassist asked the parents if they'd consider coming to work for him on his estate just outside Dublin. They accepted the offer and moved shortly thereafter, functioning as his housekeeper and driver. Eventually, they'd be promoted to his personal assistants.

Mo and I talked for four hours. Despite my fascination with the band, power and money, I was also equally interested in being friends with Mo. I didn't think I would be, but I liked him and his ideas about life. He seemed to know a lot about the power of the mind, something I was interested in.

He knew all about hypnosis. He taught himself how to play guitar within a matter of months, and the piano shortly after, with virtually no outside instruction. When Mo was a teenager, his dad taught him how to play golf. Cut to a few short years later and Mo was playing with pros as their guest on courses around the world.

This guy is fascinating. He knows how to run his mind.

As we were leaving the coffee shop, Mo suddenly had an idea.

"Right," Mo interrupted. "Let's go get you a book that will change your life. In fact, let's go get five of them. You'll need five copies."

And just like that, we sped up to Barnes and Noble in Union Square.

"What the hell is this kid rushing for," I thought.

I gasped for air, smiled approvingly at the craziness and dodged tourists.

I was 21-years-old and a sophomore at Marymount Manhattan College in New York City. I was majoring in business communications, and going through the motions toward a degree. Not-so-quietly, I was desperately seeking something bigger than the college classroom. I wanted to learn about the world, not about liberal arts and rhetoric. Mo seemed to know about the world and about people. I wanted an all-access pass to his brain.

Lavish generosity makes one curious

Mo obviously liked to set the pace. I felt excited and curious about the book, and more curious about his spastic and impulsive decision making.

We got to the bookstore. He grabbed more than five copies – he grabbed the entire fucking book shelf. It was all a bit manic, really—even for me.

"Here, take these," he instructed as he passed me a ton of books. I looked at the cover.

The Secret.

The bill at the register was over a hundred dollars. I laughed nervously, and still didn't know what I was going to do with a dozen copies of *The Secret.*

"This kid is out of his goddamn mind," I thought as frigid winter air engulfed us.

Mo told me to take as many books as I wanted and then to give the rest out to people that could use it. I did.

The frivolous generosity continued as Mo and I became friends, and I developed an unconscious desire to keep up and compete with the spending. It was very weird.

He bought our friends hundred dollar meals, car service around New York City, and his million dollar apartment was always open for guests during Mo's frequent trips back to Ireland.

Whenever I'd stay at the apartment, there were $20 and $50 bills all over the floor and even in the bathroom. It was all very surreal. Either this guy was detached from the riches in his life or extremely careless. I had never experienced anything like it.

I was hooked on the feeling of not knowing what was next. It was an adrenaline pumping-thrill of a lifetime each time Mo and I were together.

After reading *The Secret* and talking with Mo about life and business (he was remarkably fluent in both), my belief system began to change. Mo was a carefree kid my age who managed to live effortlessly and spend freely. He was who I wanted to be.

A last minute adventure

Mo had to return to his home in Europe to figure out some details for his work visa in the United States. About two weeks after he returned home, my phone rang and it was an Irish telephone number.

"Hey, Mo!" I greeted. "How are you, buddy?"

"Jake! We're going to Machu Picchu," he said without a greeting. "This week."

"Machu pich-what," I thought. *"Isn't that in South America somewhere?"*

4

"What do you mean dude," I asked.

"My girlfriend, she's going to arrive in Machu Picchu," Mo said, matter-of-factly. "She's hiking up the mountain and we need to find a way to get there before her on Thursday."

It was Monday afternoon.

"Helicopter!" Mo spouted a moment later, not giving me time to think. "Can you look into getting a helicopter to get us up the mountain in time?" he asked. "We should surprise her!"

I jotted down notes of the itinerary on the fly. I hadn't even accepted his invitation.

Sensing my hesitation, Mo peddled backwards.

"I need your help to pull this off Jake," he said, "can you help us do this? It'll be fun."

I felt like James Bond on a mission, should I choose to accept it—international locale, helicopters, Peruvian liaisons and only a few days to get it all done.

Was this real? Is he crazy?

It was finals week at Marymount Manhattan, where I was a sophomore. I was supposed to stay and do the exams. I wrestled with what I should do for a moment, and then I realized that this real-life education was more important than grades and missing a silly exam or two.

Fuck it. I'm going to Peru.

If Mo did nothing else for me and my life, he taught what it was like to literally create a new reality supported by a new belief system of what-is-possible. He insisted that people could train their mind to create the outcomes they most desire just by focusing on what was pleasing to them. I started to buy into it.

I had dreamt of living a life like this for years. It was coming true. I never thought about Peru or helicopters in Lima, but I considered what it would be like to take last minute trips, surprise friends in other countries and look rich while doing it. Mo's impulsive behavior and generosity made these daydreams suddenly become possible.

If this is possible, then what else could be possible?

Mo booked the tickets that evening. First class Continental Airlines tickets from Newark, New Jersey to Lima, Peru.

He asked me to handle the South American portion of the trip. He instructed me to coordinate with local travel bureaus for helicopter rentals, first class accommodations on the mountain and chauffeurs.

Moments later, only an hour after he first called me, the ticketed flight confirmation pinged my inbox with an inquiry.

"Jake, is everything set up in South America yet?"

The beat of our friendship was quick and without pause. He ran, I raced to keep up.

I researched everything. No detail could be left to chance. Mo's credit card was made available for all costs. I grew up believing that money didn't grow on trees and that people are never blindly generous.

They always want something in return.

Yet, Mo showed me how easily money can flow. The scarcity with which I grew up was no longer a factor in my life, at least for the moment. The way I thought about money wasn't empowering or exciting. Many people talk about what they don't have, rather than focusing on the abundance around them. I've always found that the more I talk about and love what I have, the more of what I want eventually becomes a part of my reality.

Feeling rich

For the first time in my life, I got to experience the thrill of feeling rich. Whether true or delusional, it didn't much matter. I knew that all I'd need was the chance to experience what it felt like to be rich and then I could become it. Think about it. You only need to touch the hot stove once as a kid to know what it feels like, and to know that you should never touch it again. The mind operates similarly with every other area of our life.

Following the Macchu Picchu fiasco, I became very friendly with Carrie Barrett, Mo's mom. I knew that Carrie was the financier of the trip and I knew she liked me. I planned to stay connected with the entire family. The education I got from hanging out with Mo and talking to his mom Carrie was more compelling than any college class.

Speaking of college classes, I paid for them with loans, one particular loan I'd use for my business. This is a tale of how I was…

2

CONNING MY MOM OUT OF $27,000

How the real-life education I was receiving had nothing to do with college but why I needed a college loan to pay for it (sorry mom)

Fortune knocks at every man's door once in his life, but in a good many cases the man is in a neighboring saloon and does not hear her.

— MARK TWAIN

You know the time when all that you've worked for comes down to a single moment?

Maybe it's the realization that your job is leading to a dead end, or when a relationship is over but you haven't built up the courage to breakup.

My moment occurred July 2007.

I was determined to get my TV show *The Edge with Jake Sasseville* on air. It had been moderately successful on a Fox affiliate in Maine, and since then I spent years pitching it to managers and agents, networks and media companies.

Some managers wanted to send me to VH1 to become a correspondent. Others thought Spike TV would be a perfect fit. Still others convinced me to take meetings at the emerging dark horse of media: web entertainment companies.

I didn't want to be a VH1 personality or YouTube sensation.

There was a lot of noise and it was hard to stay above it. It was satisfying to have people who "believed" in me, yet none of them believed in me enough to listen to what I wanted. I knew what I wanted and I was clear: a slot on late night television.

I made a commitment to myself: *Whatever it takes, whatever the cost, this will happen.*

In July, I took massive steps to get clear. I documented my intentions and goals. I decided to learn how to influence people instead of depending on agents. I studied human psychology, persuasion and sales techniques from Tony Robbins. I asked a ton of questions and practiced my new techniques on everyone I met.

A sales force of one

I decided that no one else was going to do this for me, and that I'd ultimately have to be the one to take charge. So I did.

I made several hundred calls a week, using the Tony Robbins method for soliciting interest and making sales. The program made sales fun, and it showed me that selling was both art and science. I was hooked.

From dawn to dusk, I "smiled and dialed." I was 20-years-old and feared getting any older while waiting for others to do the grunt work.

My plan was simple: Raise money from advertisers who wanted to market to people in their teens and 20s, hire a staff, produce an amazing show and buy my way on the air in paid programming around the country. Prove the show concept, get ratings and win an audience. Then I'd bring the show to networks with that momentum.

I learned how brutal of a world the advertising industry is as I pandered to brands to get behind a TV show that didn't exist. I was either going to get *really* good at selling thin air, or flame out before I took off.

I signed my college loan papers for the 2007-2008 academic school year. Thirty Gs. I chose to withhold information about how much my school tuition actually cost that year: $3,000. I'd re-route the $27,000 remaining to the bank account of Foot in Mouth, Inc., my production company, and use it for startup capital.

It was fairly risky, punctuated by the fact that my mom and stepfather Ray were co-signers.

They trusted me enough to use the money for school.

Yet, I was using it for a different type of schooling. It was outside the classroom and in the real world. It'd turn out to be the best, yet most painful, education ever.

Sure, I should have told my mom and Ray where the cash was actually going. But my mother was not an entrepreneur.

She wouldn't understand.

Those who are crazy enough to be an entrepreneur know that you have to make tough decisions just to stay alive. This was one of them for me. I weighed the options and determined that I had enough self-confidence that I could take the $27,000 and turn it into an investment worth the risk.

My mom was already concerned about co-signing a loan and to tell her that most of it would be used to start my business, well, that just was not possible.

Win at any cost.

I strong-armed the student loan office to write me the check personally, rather than sending it to the school (normal procedure would have the check cut to the college).

I was on a mission and tired of the old Hollywood system of pitching and praying an executive would green light a TV show for me. I'd have to figure out a way to do this outside of the system.

My mom found out where the money really went nearly two years later when I started to default on the loans. She was angrier about this than I ever imagined.

A college degree = buying a piece of real estate (minus) receiving the house

I wasn't creating anything of value in college. I wrote papers and took exams, and listened to a smart person lecture for a couple hours a week on a subject I was mildly interested in. As hard as I tried I couldn't find any real value.

I wasn't learning how to change the world, think differently, do sales or be a great marketer. I wasn't learning how to negotiate business deals or influence people who were smarter than me. I wasn't learning how to handle myself in business or the entertainment industry. At best, I'd take a senior-level course in entrepreneurship as a freshman, but was utterly bored with everything else. I'd watch as classmates would stay up all night to write a paper for a grade that in a few weeks would be recycled in a bin.

Why would I ever create something that isn't changing the world? Why would you?

I decided that the summer of 2007 was the perfect backdrop to stage my all-out assault on the entertainment industry and re-educate myself before I became apathetic to the education I was paying for in college. Big words for a kid from Maine making $250 a week, living in Queens, barely able to pay rent and conning his parents to co-sign a startup loan for his business.

I got the $30,000 check delivered that summer and paid my college the $3,000 I owed them and the rest went toward my business. And I had just begun. Because I was about to learn how...

3

MONEY DOES GROWS ON TREES (THAT ARE THEN MADE INTO FEDEX ENVELOPES)

Why the only difference between $300 and $30,000 are two zeros and a mind fuck.

*I don't know if I practiced more than anybody, but I sure practiced enough.
I still wonder if somebody — somewhere — was practicing more than me.*

— LARRY BIRD

I called every advertiser and advertising agency in America. I also was in touch with Carrie Barrett in Ireland. I picked her brain about business, assuming that her involvement with the rock band and their millions meant she had skills on how to manage large amounts of money.

I was reaching out for help and mentors in any place I could find them.

On one of my weekly calls with Carrie, things started to feel different. She was becoming interested in my work, and the vision for my TV show. She was more eager than usual to give her time.

Naturally, I was happy to share with anyone who showed interest.

It was August 2007, and I was in a deep sales cycle with the Chief Marketing Officer of Overstock.com, Stormy Simon.

"I am going to get this office space and I feel like I can convince Overstock.com to write me a check to advertise on the show," I told Carrie.

She coached me on the importance of managing money, cash flow and accounting. As I saw the Overstock.com deal come closer to fruition, I anticipated excitement and anxiety over how I'd manage all aspects of my company—hiring, accounting, producing a great show and figuring out ways to keep the money coming in.

"Carrie, do you know anyone on this side of the pond I could talk to?"

"Call this guy," she replied. She gave me a name and phone number of David Fagenson, one of the most influential investment bankers in the U.S.

"He's an Executive Vice President at Merrill Lynch and knows me from the work with the band," Carrie said.

She rattled off some information about how he helped bring Martha Stewart Living Omnimedia, Inc. and Elevation Partners public.

I thanked Carrie and called David Fagenson that afternoon. We chatted for an hour and he offered to help me but wasn't sure how he could.

I told him I understood it may be premature, and opted to keep the relationship warm rather than trying to force anything.

A surprise cash offer

The next day, Carrie called me. We exchanged greetings and she told me how impressed David Fagenson was with me. She quickly caught me off guard with a proposal.

"Well, if you need, I can come in with a few thousand dollars," she said.

I was startled by the offer, stammering to thank her as I regained my bearings.

"What did a few thousand dollars mean exactly?" I wondered.

"How much could you do with?" she asked.

Do with? Who says how much can you do with? I could do with a lot, or a little.

Shit.

"How much can you give me?" I asked, slipping on my words, trying to sound humble.

I waited on baited breathe for her answer. I would've taken anything she had to give me—$20, $200, a coupon to Duane Reade—anything.

"Would $30,000 get you started?"

Boom.

She was my genie in a bottle, offering money even at the sound of my uneasiness with her offer.

I was silent, still reeling. Carrie took it as a cue to say something more.

"If you think it could help, I could just FedEx you a check, no problem," she said with an ease in her voice. "Does that work for you?"

"Excuse me, what do you mean?" I questioned. "What do I owe you because of that?"

"Well, you'll be a rich man, so you pay me back in a few years, its fine," she said.

"You're going to, err, um, send me thirty thousand dollars tomorrow?"

"Yeah, yeah," she insisted. "I figured I could help you and just start you out and you've been such a good friend to my son that it's the least I could do."

The next morning, I was in my apartment in Queens. It was a beautiful summer day. I hadn't forgotten about the FedEx delivery, but I was in denial so I did other things. I couldn't imagine that a woman who met me once in my life would actually write me a check for $30,000.

Just then, the FedEx guy showed up with an envelope. I ripped it open without thinking. There it was. I held Carrie's signed check for $30,000 in my hand for a minute before I actually started to believe it.

As I dug through the envelope, I noticed the one page agreement that made the sum an interest-free loan, due back to Carrie in two years.

Two years? So much is going to be different in two years. No problem, I'll pay her back.

I signed and mailed the loan paper back to Carrie.

By August, 2007 I was moving at quite a clip. I was just about to do a deal with Overstock.com as my first advertiser. I had $27,000 from my college loan already in my bank account. With Carrie's thirty grand, I was in business.

I started hunting for office space instead of buying textbooks for my junior year of college. My college education was assaulting my natural, insatiable curiosity anyways.

I ran to the bank with my check in my pocket.

When I arrived, I walked to the teller, smiled and asked to deposit the check. As the teller worked, I reflected.

The real difference between rich and poor is what happens before you get there

There's no difference between a $300 check a $30,000 check.

There was no special treatment. I was the same guy wearing the same jeans and un-ironed t-shirt I wore yesterday. No one next to me knew I had thirty thousand dollars.

In fact, in the months prior, I entered that very bank and deposited several $300 checks from my part-time job at Uppereast.com, a hyper-local website for the Upper East Side of Manhattan, where I did data entry.

I've learned that big moments in my life are often preceded by big mind shifts. Leading up to the $30,000 check from Carrie, I had re-learned about money and belief systems from Mo. I became focused and deliberate with my goals, despite all the "noise" around me from managers and agents.

I've never been a "believe it when I see it" kind of person. It's so important to learn that you must believe it BEFORE you can see it, as counterintuitive as it may seem. Otherwise, you'll always be late to the game.

How often have you missed out on an opportunity because you had to "see it" first?

I walked out of the bank, ran home and called Carrie to thank her. I told her I'd invest it wisely.

"I don't care what you spend it on," she began. "Just make something worth being proud of."

"Carrie," I said. "I can't thank you enough for this. If it comes up, do you mind I share this story with the press?"

"Oh Jake, you're so kind," she quickly interrupted. "Let's keep this between you and me; I'd rather be the do-gooder behind the scenes. I don't like a lot of attention for what I do."

The generosity didn't seem suspect to me at the time. Little did I realize, at that moment, I was unknowingly getting involved with a huge million-dollar embezzlement scheme orchestrated by Carrie. It was a scheme that would continue for years and eventually land Carrie Barrett in jail.

I focused on the goodness around me and kept selling to advertisers. That's where I'd meet Stormy Simon, and found out quickly that...

4

FOR STORMY SIMON AND ME, IT'S ALL ABOUT THE O

How Overstock.com's $125,000 changed my life, why I fell in love with an alleged former exotic dancer and what my crash course in business taught me about making (and breaking) the rules.

No sale is really complete until the product is worn out, and the customer is satisfied.

– L.L. BEAN

During the summer I honed my sales skills. I completed Tony Robbins' "Mastering Influence" program and was well on the road to mastering it.

After two months of non-stop calling, pitching and being refused through the gate, I finally managed to see some light from Stormy Simon, Chief Marketing Officer at Overstock.com.

I made it a point to memorize the bios of everyone at any company I pitched. Even if I didn't receive a call back from the executive right away, I'd have notes on their lives, their families, their work histories, how much money they made and any other information I could find at my fingertips.

J. Edger Hoover didn't have shit on me.

For example, I read online that Stormy was once an exotic dancer prior to being chosen by the CEO of Overstock.com to head their marketing team in 1999. Whether true or not, I filtered info and took the most important stuff. In fact, the more I learned about these people, the more I began to like them—allowing me to authentically connect with them on the rare occasion they'd answer the phone or an email.

The following is the initial email I sent to Stormy—verbatim—using the Tony Robbins system:

Dear_____,

I can deliver _____ (something very personal/something valuable to them). What this means for you is _____ (give them something that it means to them emotionally). What this really means to you _____ (reaffirm that point with a complimentary, logical point.)

The reason I say that is because _____ (give a because statement).

Call me.

The word "because" justifies any part of the aforementioned. It's a four-sentence email that raises eyebrows. Some would write back, few called, but I was getting my share of NO THANK YOUs.

My skin thickened for the most part, but Stormy Simon called me back and softened me up.

My first encounter with a Chief Marketing Officer

When Stormy and I finally connected on the phone, business was the last thing on the agenda. We spoke about life, our dreams and our difficult growing pains. She lost her sister years before, just as I had lost my thirteen year old brother. I loved my connection with Stormy! We talked for hours.

This lesson was a part of the education I was pursuing. It taught me that business can be personal and extraordinarily creative. In college, the only thing I learned about business was case studies and how others had done it. With the exception of one innovative entrepreneurship course taught by former Jim Henson executive Isabelle Miller at Marymount, none of my college courses taught me how to create greatness.

"Why don't you come to LA next week," Stormy invited at the end of our fifth phone chat. "We're shooting our Super Bowl commercial and I'd like you to meet our CEO and my branding team."

I accepted the invite and bought tickets to Los Angeles on my credit card.

After a twelve-hour day on the set of their Super Bowl XLII commercial (a game that would be the biggest upset in NFL history between the Giants and the Patriots), Stormy invited me back to the hotel to meet the CEO and Founder of Overstock.com, Patrick Byrne. She told me her marketing director Nicole Bondoc would also be there.

Meeting of the minds with people I'd appreciate for a lifetime

After exchanging niceties, Stormy sat back and let Patrick and Nicole grill me.

"You're going to get on ABC how?" Patrick asked with a furrowed brow.

Patrick was a tall, robust man with broad shoulders. This came as a shock. My research about Patrick suggested that he was a bit frailer. He survived cancer several times, and had gone on to bicycle across the United States on several occasions. I was inspired to meet him. I realized I still had yet to answer his question.

"I'm going to buy my way on the air and produce one hell of a show," I said, matter-of-factly.

"How much does that cost," Nicole interrupted.

"A few thousand dollars a week."

"But you've only asked us for $125,000," Patrick said. "How are you going to raise the rest?"

"I have hundreds of other deals in the pipeline," I insisted. "I just need my first YES."

I paused and glanced away for a moment, only to return to lock eyes with Patrick.

"I just need my first YES from you, Patrick."

And that was absolutely true. I just needed to know what one YES would feel like.

Isn't that what we all need? Some sort of validation that what we're doing is justified?

Stormy looked concerned, realizing that if she said YES, she'd be my first.

I quickly filled the silence.

"The biggest rock band in the world has already invested money," I exaggerated, "and I just need an advertiser who stands up and says 'I believe.'"

"What happens if you can't raise the rest of the money?" Patrick asked "What happens to our investment?"

"I don't fail, Patrick," I said.

I had nothing to fail at up to that point. First time for everything.

Fail quickly

I know so many entrepreneurs who are filled with great ideas and undeniable genius. Yet their point of view is one-sided mainly because they never experienced what it feels like to fail.

When I hire people I implore them to please fail as quickly as possible up front so that they can move onto bigger and better things. Some look at me like I'm out of my mind, and I usually don't hire them. Other's eyes light up and they feel relief, and those are the folks I want.

I confidently weaved the perception that I had everything under control. In reality, I felt totally out of control. I was terrified of adding another NO to a pile of hundreds.

Nicole Bondoc peppered me with questions about how Overstock.com could reach a younger demo and what the company could be doing better.

It appeared that she was already using me as a consultant, and I relished the opportunity to help.

Still, I was curious what was happening on the other side of the room with Patrick and Stormy.

I could see Patrick leaning in towards Stormy, whispering.

"I don't know who this kid is Stormy, but he has some huge balls," Patrick mumbled. "I'll let you do whatever you think is best."

Just then, Patrick interrupted my conversation with Nicole.

"Jake, pleasure to meet you, I have to go to bed," he said.

I stood up and thanked him sincerely for taking the time to meet with me.

"Thank you for believing in me Patrick," I said as we shook hands. "I'm looking forward to creating great things together."

Assume the sale. I didn't know how I'd do it, but I believed in every pore of my body that I could make Overstock.com happy. So why not say it?

Two weeks later, and after a flurry of questions from Overstock.com headquarters in Salt Lake, Stormy and Nicole called me and told me that they were in.

"Good," Stormy said. "We're doing this."

HOLY SHIT.

"Thank you, thank you, thank you," I endlessly professed. "You won't regret this. I promise!"

We hung up. And Overstock.com wrote me a check for $59,000 the next day.

A realization about following your dream

Overstock.com and Stormy Simon were my first.

Granted, it would be the first of many, but for the kid with a dream of owning his own TV studio and production company in the entertainment business and being a force in the industry, this was a true confirmation that I was on my way.

You see, it was a small amount of money for Overstock.com, a company with an annual advertising budget of more than $50 million. They probably did it because they liked me more than anything else. But after years of being told NO and still hanging on to *what could be*, this was a defining moment.

I had been to Los Angeles to meet with agents, managers, networks and casting directors a dozen times before I hit legal drinking age.

Everyone told me NO.

Overstock.com saw my vision and told me YES. Hundreds of NOs for one YES? I'll take it.

The level of determination was born from a deep desire to succeed. I think a big piece of it was my age – things you learn when you're a teenager stick with you.

At 13, I was flopping and failing in front of hundreds of people as I did my magic tricks from stage. Magic taught me how to conceal my mistakes with dialog. It also taught me that making mistakes is actually more interesting than getting it right.

Imagine: Making mistakes is *more* **interesting** than getting it right.

In this way, I activated parts of my psychology to perceive challenges and adversity as simply more interesting instead of something to fear.

And you can, too. If how you perceive the world isn't serving you, re-frame it. I've been told by dozens of people that my threshold for pain, disappointment and failure is uncharacteristically high. It's because I <u>believe</u> without a doubt that failures bring success and richness to my life. So I welcome the failures, because the successes are fun, and they are always around the corner.

Hard times (but you'd never know it)

Interestingly, at the time of this writing (December 2011), if not for the generosity of one of my best friends, I wouldn't have had the money in my bank account to buy food and eat today. I had $1.18 in my bank account and my friend gave me $200. This, coming from a guy that has hundred thousand dollar proposals in front of major corporations and who's business made one million dollars the year prior.

Still, at the time of the seventh edit of this book (July 2012), my business has generated several hundred thousand dollars in the last few months alone. I'm on the other side of that same proverbial coin. And it's all happened in a few short months.

Do you see that it's not about the amount of money but rather the level of focus you have?

Things change and you have to go with the flow and keep your eye on the prize. Choose your prize wisely. My point here is that I've had many downturns in my career and my life. This most recent one had left me dry for roughly eight months. Even so, I refuse to look for a job and I refuse to stop trying. I hung on, and learned a ton in the process.

I'd argue I'm not unique. I'd argue that if you want something bad enough in this life, you too can create a belief system that will not allow you to fail. It's not my set of circumstances that dictate whether or not I choose to continue firing on all cylinders. It's how I choose to look at those circumstances. And how you choose to look at the circumstances in your life *create* your life.

Creating a big life is not the problem. Growing a big business isn't the problem. What becomes an issue is when you get...

5

TOO BIG, TOO FAST

Why I fired my assistant after two weeks (and why you should too), hire the best as quickly as you can, and, above all else: do everything backwards, at least in the beginning.

If power is for sale, sell your mother to buy it. You can always buy her back again.

— ARABIC PROVERB

I hired an assistant a week after the Overstock.com sent me $59,000.

The assistant, Marcie, made critical errors on an accounting spread-sheet and worse, she didn't own up to it. Perhaps I was asking her to do too much, or she was incompetent.

Either way, I didn't want to wait to find out. She had to go.

I brought her into our conference room and explained my reasons for letting her go. She was eating pineapple slices. I'll never forget how her face dropped before sobbing at the table. She was shocked that I'd fire her. I tried to be as tender as I could, but it didn't work. She was two years older than me (I was 22), and she resented my decision.

She stormed out of the room. Outraged.

Some people just aren't made for startups.

After firing my first assistant, I hired Sasha Ramirez, a Syracuse University graduate who was calm, cool, collected, organized and dedicated. Hiring a competent assistant is key.

The reason I hired an assistant is because of what I read about Richard Branson, and his assistant Penni Pike. Penni stayed with Richard from the beginning and dedicated twenty-six years to helping steer Richard's Virgin billion-dollar empire.

She never asked for a promotion and was the rock in Richard's life. I was inspired by this and wanted to replicate it. (I'm still trying to find "the one" five years later!)

Calling Richard Branson

Hell, I was so in awe by Penni Pike that I tracked her down on the houseboat Branson gave her shortly before she retired. It was docked off the River Thames in London. We spoke briefly and I shared with her how much her story inspired me to be the best entrepreneur I could be. She was gracious and agreed to pass a message to Richard Branson on my behalf.

I made sure my team heard the whole conversation. I wanted that conversation to set the pace for the enormous expectations that I had for them.

That "team" was made up of fresh faced twenty-somethings – Brian Burstein, an NYU sophomore studying TV, Sasha and my best friend, Manuel Rappard, an NYU senior studying business from Germany. To describe us as novices is an understatement; equally, though, we were energized and gleefully making up <u>all</u> the rules as we went.

Hiring the best

Weeks after receiving the check from Overstock.com, I only hired young, hungry and interesting people because they didn't ask questions and leaped at the opportunity to splash around and get messy. "Serious" people don't do this as much. They have too much to watch out for, too much to lose. Not the folks I hired.

Thinking too critically about a decision can botch a delicate business maneuver. Intuitively I understood this, and stayed away from dwelling on any one thing for too long. Sack up and trust that you can do it.

Young, hungry and interesting people were more willing to toss aside the script and make it up. That thrilled me. And I know it thrilled them, too. There was such joy and eagerness in our work. It was the lifeline of our fledgling organization. And it was all I needed to keep my energy high.

We settled into a beautiful TriBeCa loft outfitted with all the essentials that sprawled over 10,000 square feet. After flexing my growing negotiating muscle with the landlord, she added six big offices, a common area, a kitchen, reception area and Wi-Fi – all for a third of her asking price. We furnished our trendy office with Salvation Army fixtures. It was absurd, delusional and yet somehow, made perfect sense.

Fake it till you make it (or just make it so you don't have to fake it)

I started interviewing for producers and writers. When I couldn't decide between two of the executive producers I wanted to hire, I hired them both.

"Who cares, I can create anything," I thought. *"I can create magic. I can create money out of thin air."*

Right or wrong, this was the belief system governing my decisions in the early days. It sounds crazy, but even crazier, people bought into it.

The main executive producer was Lori Fitch, a renowned TV showrunner in LA and NY. She also was a production executive in the 90s at NBC.

The vision was simple, if not naïve: There was nothing on TV after *Jimmy Kimmel Live* in many markets, except for paid programming. I could go to dozens of cities and buy the 30-minute airtime after Jimmy Kimmel and insert *The Edge with Jake Sasseville* instead of a regular paid program, as long as *The Edge* met FCC requirements.

It was a pipe dream filled with heart, and just enough street smarts to be possible. We knew we needed a hook to get people excited.

The certainty that comes with belief in self

One thing I did exceptionally well in the early days was I encouraged those around me to believe that they were much more powerful than they actually were. I couldn't afford the people who were actually powerful. So, I made my freshman hires believe they were unstoppable. And sure enough, together, we became unstoppable.

As much as I enjoyed the thrill of starting my own business, I equally feared losing it all. Almost immediately after receiving my first check from Overstock.com, the fears of *what-if* began. I saw costs rising and people coming in for interviews. I didn't know how I'd pay for it all.

Empowering the troops

I needed a talented stable of writers to sculpt my brand of funny for the masses.

My head writer, Katie Bashinelli, was seasoned. Her resume was teeming with 15 years of experience, including a successful number of years at "Chappelle's Show." I hired her immediately, and asked that she, in turn, hire her writing team. Immediately.

"Shouldn't that be your producer's job?" she asked, unfamiliar with my protocol, and not even contracted yet.

"Maybe, but now it's your job," I replied. "Make it happen. I'll send the contract to you soon."

I was focused and deliberate, if not bordering on immodest and tactless. Since I was a teen, I practiced putting myself in the most uncomfortable situations and finding my way out without a safety net.

I daydreamt about running a business in entertainment for years. The corner office loft in New York City, a staff catering to my whimsical ideas and a pace of work that'd make an MBA's head spin were what I dreamed about every day. And now I was living it.

I had a staff of ten by September 2007. Assistants, producers, writers and the few recently hired technical crew members rounded out the team.

One of the crucial mistakes I made was not putting together a *business* team. I thought I could do it alone. I was still doing all the sales for the company while my assistant Sasha dedicated three hours of her afternoon to cold calls (any time she reached someone important, she'd grab me and I'd pitch on a whim).

Adrenaline skyrocketed as Sasha made the announcements, often interrupting meetings or brainstorm sessions.

"Jake, I have the vice president of marketing for Dunkin Donuts." Sasha would yell. "Patching him thru, you ready?"

Then I began with my pitch. It was less of a pitch and more of a stream-of-consciousness dialog about whatever was on my mind that day, with the intention of opening up the conversation to get the prospective buyer to talk about what it is they were really wanting.

How's that for sales 2.0? At least it was entertaining for the people on the other line.

I remember how confused Tony Post, CEO of Vibrams USA (the five fingers shoes), was when my assistant patched him through.

"Um, hello, who is this?" Tony asked.

"TV's Jake Sasseville, Tony, nice to meet you," I said without hesitation.

"Jake?" Tony inquired, not knowing who I was.

"Yes!" I said, as if we had known each other for years.

I stuck with every awkward moment, and Tony and I had a great conversation.

Years later Tony and I remain friends and have done business together. Anyone who sees me can attest I wear Vibrams faithfully, and have since day one.

I did the accounting, bookkeeping, cashed the checks and cleaned the office. In a few weeks' time, I'd have to start hosting the show we were creating. My days started early and ended late.

I instructed Katie, my head writer, to begin drafting thirteen episodes for the show. We still didn't know what the show would be. We knew it'd feature me as host in situations and with celebrity guests. We knew we'd use New York City as the backdrop, but that was the extent of it.

What 'situations'? What 'guests'?

Backwards thinking frustrates the troops. Get clear. Quick.

My process to produce a successful late night TV show was completely upside down. I had never done it before so I figured, at worst, I'd create an interesting TV show and, at best, I'd start a revolution. I was happy with either.

Aborting the mission was never an option, no matter how tough it got. Some mornings after my writer's meetings all I wanted to do was take a nap. (And the only thing my head writer Katie wanted to go back and work for Comedy Central.)

The problem was with me. I was the bottleneck. I pitched a clear vision, but when the creative drilling started, we came up empty. In fact, not only did we miss the oil, but suddenly, after we'd be drilling for weeks, I'd change my idea about the field entirely.

I didn't know what type of show I wanted to create. I'd say one thing, and then change my mind a week later. You can imagine that trying to read your bosses mind in an already chaotic and stressed startup environment is frustrating at best.

I had to convince my creative team that we'd have to push ourselves to accept that we weren't going to know exactly what was being created, but to trust that it was going to be our best work. After weeks of pretending that I knew what I wanted, I finally admitted that I didn't have a clue what I'd be good at, but that I'd know it when I saw it.

This drove the staff nuts, but they stuck with me. When you don't know the answer, as the leader, you must carefully articulate that you don't know. Do so from a place of strength.

We decided that turning the cameras on ourselves and our process would not only be entertaining, but also educational for our audience. Once I started to embrace my own flaws as a leader, we started to embrace our challenges as a late night TV show. We all felt something very interesting was about to happen.

(In terms of both ratings and content, to date, *The Edge with Jake Sasseville*, season one is one of my best TV products I've ever produced and I think everything above is the reason why.)

Do what you know, take chances on what you don't, trust your instincts no matter who fights you on it. Move by faith not by sight. Even if it doesn't work or if you make mistakes, it's a hell of a fun ride.

A culture copycat

I created a company culture inspired by other companies I loved.

I didn't set hours. My staff usually still worked 12-hour days.

I didn't mandate how many sick days people could have, and miraculously, no one ever took one.

I didn't tell anyone how long they had for lunch, and we had great 2-hour lunches on the roof, overlooking the Hudson River.

I told them to go on vacations as they pleased so long as they could juggle their work with another person. They rarely left for days off.

I got these ideas from companies like Virgin and Google, but intuitively as a human being, these ideas made sense. In reality, it made my staff very happy and enthusiastic about life and work.

People brought friends to the office to hang out. One day I was editing a segment and Donnie Wahlberg (*New Kids on the Block*) was sitting in a chair next to one of my producers (they were friends). I was oblivious to who he was, but the women enjoyed themselves.

My generation is one of the first generations to "live out loud." From status updates to anti-bullying videos on YouTube, we emulate those who came before us and create our world out of it. And it would be my generation that would be instrumental in the ...

6

BIRTH OF THE "JAKE AFTER JIMMY ON ABC" CAMPAIGN

The more <u>personal</u> a marketing campaign is, the more <u>universal</u> it is. (just make sure the product doesn't suck).

Genius is no more than childhood recaptured at will, childhood equipped now with man's physical means to express itself, and with the analytical mind that enables it to bring order into the sum of experience, involuntarily amassed.

— Charles Baudelaire

I learned from Steve Jobs that you always consider how a product or idea will be marketed *before* you spend too much time creating the product.

33

"I want my Jake after Jimmy on ABC" was created with this in mind.

I knew I had to start marketing *The Edge with Jake Sasseville* before we created the show. I knew that once we figured out the messaging, that all the hiccups with the creation of *The Edge* would diminish.

This might sound counterintuitive, but operating outside the status quo was quickly becoming my forte. And I promise it will make sense once you read the whole story.

Sasha, Manuel and Brian were sitting in our office on a beautiful September afternoon.

Brian did everything from production to leading our digital team and negotiating with the ABC network TV affiliates in cities around the US. He was a stickler for details, and exasperated me with his constant barrage of questions and *what-if* scenarios, forcing me to think through everything. Brian kept us focused, humble and honest. The fact that he was 19 years old and an NYU sophomore made the story even better.

Manuel was becoming one of my best friends. We met at a party earlier in the year and talked for hours. We'd spend long nights together ideating on philosophy, to relationships, to business and philanthropy. He did strategy and figured out how to execute our ideas. He also filled in the gaps anywhere he could.

Manuel and me enjoying San Francisco together.

Sasha was my right hand woman who communicated with everyone on the outside world. She handled questions and concerns by staff, helped me with accounting and scheduling, helped me hire and fire people and kept the business teeming.

The three of them made up my inner circle in those early days. I relied on them for everything.

The four of us sat mesmerized as we tried to figure out how we'd create a show that people wanted to watch, and a marketing campaign that would support it.

I had a commitment to Overstock.com to air on *at least* 20 ABC stations. I sold in the "after Kimmel" idea without creating the "I want my Jake after Jimmy on ABC" campaign. It felt right, but I hadn't made the connection when I first met Stormy.

We knew that going on after *Jimmy Kimmel Live* meant 1:00 a.m. timeslots for the majority of the country. The missing piece (and there were many missing pieces) was how to get people to know that we were on after Jimmy Kimmel.

Good ideas turning great

During a break after my writer's meeting, I blurted out to Sasha and Brian "JAKE AFTER JIMMY."

"Guys, what if we create a campaign that makes it look like we "won" our way on the air," I said.

Manuel was intrigued. Brian was more skeptical.

"What do you mean 'campaign?'?" Brian asked. "Like a petition?"

"Yes," I insisted. "Let's create the 'I Want My Jake after Jimmy on ABC' campaign."

The group got excited.

I reminded them how "I want my MTV" in the 1980s was a generational call-to-action. Perhaps this was the 21st century's version of that media plea. If we could buy time on 20 ABC stations as "social proof" and create the "Jake after Jimmy" campaign around it, maybe we could make a much bigger dent in the television industry.

"Sasha, go buy the domain JakeafterJimmy.com immediately," I said.

Sasha reached to the floor to get her laptop. Furniture was scarce and she donated her desk to the writers.

"Brian, what if we build a site driving people to e-petition ABC executives locally," I suggested.

"And we could have a blind copy to go ABC executives in Los Angeles," Brian said.

"And send one to Jimmy Kimmel's producers too," Sasha said as she clicked *Purchase* on our new domain name at GoDaddy.com.

Essentially, we'd create a map of the United States on JakeafterJimmy. com, fill in 20 states where we'd buy time after Kimmel, give users the option to click on a state, and if we weren't on that local ABC affiliate, a form would pop up that the user could fill out and click *Submit*.

The BCC field in the email would blast to ABC, Kimmel and the local TV stations.

It was a renegade, novel idea for disrupting the system.

Manuel interrupted the flow, if only for a moment.

"It's a good idea, but you need to hit critical mass," Manuel said. "A few emails to ABC executives will not work and will fail."

Fail.

It was the one four-letter word I detested. I cringe at the thought of failing. All of this was already too damn good to be true anyways.

But Manuel was right.

No one knew who I was. Our business was a startup with a tiny bit of cash and a sales force of one.

I couldn't afford commercials or to do expensive grassroots marketing. It had to be simple. It had to be scalable. It had to be cheap.

Once the idea is there, begin immediately

We broke for lunch and I called Tara, my publicist, for our weekly check in. (You probably shouldn't hire a publicist before you hire an accountant—another lesson learned.)

Tara owned her own public relations firm in Atlanta. She'd be the first of eight publicists I'd hire and fire over the course of the next four years.

"Jake," Tara said, her southern accent almost preceding her. "I just got off the phone with Max Duncan. Max works at Crocs' marketing department and they're putting on a fall tour with the band Guster."

Tara was talking about the Crocs Next Step Campus Tour. The tour was scheduled to travel to top universities that semester."

"Guster," I said. "Guster is great. I used to listen to them in high school."

"I talked you up to Max and he wants to speak with you," Tara said.

"Tara, what does he want specifically?"

"Well, what do you think about hosting the tour this fall? It starts in a few weeks," she said. "And Kanye West is scheduled to be on it as well."

Wait a minute! Could this be happening?

"They won't pay you, but..."

I cut her off.

"Tara, never mind about paying me. Give me Max's phone number please."

This Tara woman might actually be worth her $3,000 a month retainer after all.

Two seconds later, I rang Max.

"Max Duncan," he answered in that deep all-American accent.

"Hello, Max. It's Jake Sasseville here. How are you?"

"Jake! I've been expecting your call. What can you do for me?"

My offer was simple.

"Put me on your tour, as your emcee, don't pay me a dime and just let me talk about my sponsor, Overstock.com. I'll take as much time on stage as you give me and I'll take care of my expenses."

And, oh yeah, let me talk about my "Jake after Jimmy" campaign.

Max took a moment to think about it.

"I'll call you back," Max said. "I have to talk with my partner."

Thirty minutes later, we had Max's commitment.

I hung up the phone and ran back into my office. Our first stop on the tour was St. Louis University in less than two weeks.

Celebrations lead to more work

"Guys, you're never going to believe it!" I exclaimed.

We worked all night planning our attack. We only had ten days to pull it off.

I called Overstock.com and asked for them to donate high-priced electronic items to give away as prizes. They immediately agreed.

I found a website that did personalized fortune cookies. Why fortune cookies? For the same reason we were doing everything else – it was a fun idea, outrageous and would get people talking.

"Manuel, we need to order 10,000 personalized fortune cookies," I said. Every fortune featured the same line:

"GO TO JAKEAFTERJIMMY.COM TO BE A PART OF THE REVOLUTION."

By midnight, 10,000 fortune cookies were ordered, Overstock.com had committed ten thousand dollars of product and Brian led our web team on a strategy to drive e-petitions to ABC.

We hadn't even produced a single episode of *The Edge with Jake Sasseville* and already the promotion gears were clicking on all cylinders.

This is going to be some ride.

The following week, 40 boxes of fortune cookies arrived at my office.

First stop: St. Louis.

"What the hell is the plan?" I asked Manuel as we stepped on the flight to St. Louis. We ideated for days on what to do with the prizes and how to drive people to JakeafterJimmy.com but nothing stuck. It was still up in the air.

The website got built just in time, and we were ready to drive traffic. But how? You can't just tell people to go to a website.

I got a sobering call from Lori Fitch , my trusty executive producer, who alerted me that I had less than a month left before I ran out of money.

Lori picks the best times to call.

I thanked Lori and hung up the phone. I told Manuel. I treated him like a business partner even though he made it clear he had no interest in being partners.

Manuel reaffirmed what I already knew. We couldn't worry about the money. Instead, we had to figure out what the big idea was in St. Louis and how we were going to drive people to JakeAfterJimmy.com. My career in television was counting on this. And more importantly, so was my staff.

An empowering idea with arms and legs makes a small dent in the universe

Just then, Manuel started speaking.

"You have all these prizes from Overstock, right?"

I nodded.

"Let's put you in front of people all day in St. Louis, treat it like a presidential campaign," Manuel said. "Hit 'em with the talking points to get them excited."

I smiled. I was so grateful for Manuel.

"While you are out talking to people, I'll find four cardboard boxes," he continued.

"We'll plaster
JAKE
AFTER
JIMMY
.COM
on each box, with Overstock.com logos."

"Then we'll blow up hundreds of colorful helium balloons," Manuel said. "Each color will represent a prize from Overstock."

"A color coded game!" I blurted out with a laugh. I was starting to get excited.

"We'll pick four people from the audience to come on stage and pick a box and three of them will be instant winners." Manuel said. "The final fourth box will have red balloons in them."

The red balloons signaled that person had a chance to win the grand prize—a 50-inch flat screen TV from Overstock.com. The red balloons also signaled a challenge to the student body.

"They'll have to get their peers to become a fan of the Facebook page we'll create specifically for that university," Manuel said. "The kid who has the most university-Likes will win the flat screen."

Brilliantly simple.

Each person who got red balloons would have a one-in-fifteen chance of winning the 50-inch flat screen. And, it'd turn into competition between school would vote the most.

It was a matter of school pride.

The plane landed just as we landed on our big idea.

Would it work?

I called Brian back at the office in New York.

"Brian," I said. "I need you to create a 'Jake after Jimmy' Facebook page for every university on this tour."

This is Brian and I in our tiny office, after we moved out of TriBeCa and into our SoHo office.

We rushed to St. Louis University and went to work. We had a staff of 10 volunteers on the ground that day thanks to Sasha and Craigslist.

As I arrived on campus I ran into Max Duncan and the other tour producers. I thanked them profusely.

The producers did some quality control and asked what I planned to do with my stage time.

"Some comedy and some giveaways," I said. "No biggie."

Meanwhile, we started seeing our "Jake after Jimmy" t-shirts showing up on random students in the quad.

We stirred St. Louis University into frenzy. I told them about the concert and I got them excited about the "Jake after Jimmy" campaign. I ambushed university classes, and hung out in the campus cafeterias.

Whatever it takes.

We filmed everything and attracted a ton of attention.

Five thousand people were expected to show up at the concert that night.

Manuel came up to me and was going through last minute preparations of how it would all play out. The sun was setting.

Then, we both looked each other and said: "Fuck it. Let's just have a great time."

We laughed about how we pulled this off in a matter of hours.

I was nervous about going on stage. I had nothing to say.

As thousands of kids started to file into the concert area, I reflected at how hard I worked so hard for this moment. I was finally in a position to do what I did best – entertain and engage people. Sometimes you can spend years working toward one single moment of opportunity.

I almost forgot that the real work of entertaining had to be done, despite the tens of thousands of hours of work and years of pushing forward that no one ever saw.

This was now my moment.

Being as flexible as water

"Jake, change of plans," Max, the producer, yelled. "You have to do your act at the top of the show, no more time in between acts."

Quickly with Manuel, we re-organized our team to go on stage in the next few moments.

"Jake!" the stage manager screamed. "Go, go, go!"

In an industry all about timing, I missed my cue. The lights were up and all attention was on an empty stage.

There were 5,000 screaming St. Louis University students in front of me.

I went for it. I went for it with all I had.

"Good Evvveeeeennnnniinngggg, St. Louis!" I exclaimed.

I started talking; stuff just came out of my mouth. I started with something easy like school pride.

"We were originally supposed to go to Wash U," I said, cueing the boos. "But I said 'I don't want to go to no Washington University.'"

Washington University was chief rival and across town from St. Louis University. It seemed like an easy way to start.

"I need your help to seal the deal with late night talk show," I invoked, explaining my plight to get on ABC.

Cheers. I couldn't believe it. Real cheers.

I united the crowd by defining our generation as the one to re-write all the rules, certainly in TV, but also in every area of life. That was, as I saw it, the core of our generational identity.

I admitted that for me it was just a television show that I had always dreamed of, but if we could pull this off, it would be a generational win about what we can do together.

Then, I picked four random people out of the crowd, explained the rules of my Overstock.com game and that each would win prizes, instantly. The crowd went nuts.

One by one, balloons came out.

Green balloons, digital camera.

Blue balloons, a new computer.

Yellow balloons, iPod.

And then, out came the red balloons.

The audience went wild.

I explained that in order to win the 50-inch flat screen the contestant would have to rally and get all his friends at St. Louis University to become a fan of the *Jake after Jimmy St. Louis University* Facebook page.

"Now, as for you guys," I turned toward the audience. "You don't want the kid at University of Florida to win, do you?"

The crowd feedback was unanimous.

"And you guys don't want the kid at University of Texas to win the big screen, doooooyouuuuuuuuuuuuuu?"

The boos got louder.

"Go to JakeafterJimmy.com right now and make sure St. Louis University wins!" I shouted.

I took a breath.

As I started to leave the stage, I remembered one last thing.

"Oh yeah, one more thing. Anybody high?" I asked.

Cheers everywhere. Offstage, the producers weren't impressed.

"Well, before I go, I have something for you," I said with a smile.

"Ladies," I commanded to our army of volunteers. "Give it to 'em."

Ten beautiful women came out with bags of fortune cookies, hurling them into the crowd. Crackling and crunching started.

On the fortune inside: "Go to JakeafterJimmy.com."

The audience from the point of view of backstage at one of the tour stops.

Opening to a crowd of thousands

I had never done a day of standup in my life. Most people my age were working comedy clubs all around the country trying to make it. Thing is, I knew I wasn't a stand-up comedian. I was a showman at best, and figured out how to mass-market a concept.

I didn't like the regular path to success. It's too crowded. I love being competitive, but would rather elevate above the fray. Instead of being one out of a million, I'd rather be one out of ten.

There have always been funnier, better looking, smarter people than me in my business. Yet, I win because I'm willing to fail. And I win because I'm simply more persistent than the rest.

The only reason I kicked my career in high gear that night and opened in front of 5,000 people was because I believed in the *business* of entertainment. I'm a businessman. No, Jay-Z, I'm a Business. Man.

I don't buy into being a starving artist or a starving anything. If you're one of a million, then you'll be treated as such. But if you distinguish yourself as a business, the world shifts to your advantage and you become one of one.

Meanwhile, I waved goodbye and ran offstage. Guster was walking out of their tour bus. I was met by the producer.

"I don't know what you just did, but amazing job Jake!" he said.

Manuel gave me a huge hug. We had done it. We actually pulled it off. Now let's see if people would actually go to JakeafterJimmy.com.

Backstage at one of the concert stops in Tennessee. One Republic is playing their hit song *Apologize* in the background

Encore

I was thanking our team of volunteers offstage. Just then, I heard a quiet murmur from the crowd.

JAKE! JAKE! JAKE! JAKE! JAKE! JAKE! JAKE!

They were chanting my name.

What?! I must be hearing things?

The producer came to me again, frazzled.

"Jake I tried to quiet them down, but they just won't shut up," he snarled. "Hurry up though, we're running late."

Hurry up to do what?!

I approached the stage. The chants were louder now. Thunderous applause started in the front of the crowd and spread all around the field. Something infected the crowd.

I thanked them and decided to be honest, since I had no "material."

"I just want to take a moment to thank you for being so supportive of us today St. Louis," I said. "This is an emotional day for me and my team, and I'll never forget that this was the city it all started in!"

Replicating success by keeping it simple

We repeated the same shtick over the next several weeks all around the country. The crowd loved it, and in some cases, word of what we were doing spread on Facebook in advance of our arrival.

It was, however, simple enough of an idea to execute. And it was scalable (we could do it in any given city and on campuses everywhere).

Most importantly, I didn't hold back because it was "different" or "challenging" to get off the ground. We committed fully, even though we didn't know all the answers. We put ourselves out there, even if it meant our flaws being exposed.

The "Jake after Jimmy" campaign helped us because it framed the conversation around my talk show, of which a few segments had been produced. Suddenly people were interested in the movement and the ideas around the movement. The Campaign sparked curiosity of what *The Edge* might be. The TV show was important, but the conversation that was happening around the TV show was far more important.

Best-selling author Seth Godin talks about "shipping it." In other words, stop finding things wrong with your idea. Instead of burying it and wondering "what-if?" bring it to the masses and see if the planning, preparations, sweat, blood and tears pays off.

If it doesn't, start over again. If it does, celebrate, and continue. Rinse and repeat.

(An interesting aside: Because we focused on promoting "Jake after Jimmy" in all our materials and t-shirts, many people thought the show's actual name was "Jake after Jimmy" and not *The Edge with Jake Sasseville*.

We never imagined this would happen, however, we didn't fight it. We decided that as long as people were remembering "Jake after Jimmy" and talking about it, that we could make the correction later. A lesson in being deliberate about what you bring to market.)

That night I went to sleep in the hotel room at around 3 a.m. I had a 6 a.m. flight. I tossed and turned all night. When I got up, I remembered the call I received from Lori Fitch a few days before, telling me that I'd run of money if I didn't figure out a solution. I was about to have...

7

MY FIRST COME-TO-JESUS-MOMENT

The 4 a.m. (Irish) Wakeup Call, Raising $60,000 Overnight, and Why Lunching With Your Staff When You Run Out of Money is Essential

The profession of a prostitute is the only career in which the maximum income is paid to the newest apprentice. It is the one calling in which at the beginning the only exertion is that of self-indulgence; all the prizes are at the commencement. It is the ever-new embodiment of the old fable of the sale of the soul to the Devil. The tempter offers wealth, comfort, excitement, but in return the victim must sell her soul, nor does the other party forget to exact his due to the uttermost farthing.

— WILLIAM BOOTH

The schedule on the road was hectic, but I never missed a writers' meeting. Like clockwork, I called my office first thing in the morning to go over the every detail of the script and production.

Success takes discipline.

The biggest concert of the tour came toward its finale.

Vanderbilt University.

10,000 tickets sold.

Kanye West performs.

...and the star of a fledgling late night talk show who no one knew hosted the concert.

Jake after Jimmy starts to stick

The "Jake after Jimmy" campaign was moving the dial. We were clearing 1:00 a.m. timeslots on local ABC stations after Jimmy Kimmel all around the country, far above the number of 20 ABC stations we initially promised Overstock.com. One month in, we hit 25 million households. It was working and station managers in cities around the United States appreciated the novelty of our approach.

Everything was falling into place.

Shit hits the fan

Lori Fitch, my trusty executive producer, warned me for weeks that I was going to run out of money. I told her that everything was fine, despite the fact that she had the budget and I didn't.

I assured her Ford Motor Company would sign soon.

After a speech at NYU, I walked from Union Square to my office in TriBeCa to find my assistant Sasha waiting at the door.

"Jake," she sulked. Her voice was almost a whisper and she was clearly concerned.

"What's going on Sasha?" I demanded.

Sasha's a horrible poker player. I could tell by the look on her face that something was desperately wrong.

"Jake, you have sixty thousand dollars in payroll to meet tomorrow," Sasha informed me.

"No problem, right? How much do we have in the account right now?" I asked.

"You're overdrawn $3,600 in your account, and you have nothing in your personal account to cover this," Sasha said.

Panic set in and my palms started to sweat. All the warning signs were in place. Lori warned me for a weeks and I had missed calls from Citibank. Lori and Sasha were the only two people who had access to the finances.

In the weeks prior, every time Sasha talked to me about the bank account, I brushed it off, letting her know that it was all going to be fine.

I got lost in the fanfare of doing shows with Kanye West and producing television that I thought the finances would "magically" work themselves out.

"Who else knows about this Sasha?" I inquired, as I sat at my computer.

She told me she was the only one. Hiring publicists, producers and writers before accountants and bookkeepers was about to bite me in the ass.

I needed a moment.

My belief system was so wound up with winning at any cost that any slight (or major) derailment didn't paralyze me. I flung into action.

I did a double take, as if waking up from a daydream.

"Sasha, what a great opportunity," I said with a smile that rivaled the Cheshire Cat. I got up from my desk, manically pacing back and forth.

"We're going to fix this and it's going to be fun!"

Her smile relieved me.

In the perils of financial meltdown

I went to my executive office down the hall.

"I don't know how this happened," I said to Lori Fitch, executive producer of *The Edge with Jake Sasseville*. Lori was like a mother to me. I was so exhausted pretending that everything was all right.

I asked Lori for business support and ideas, but she gently said that she was not interested getting involved in the business side of things.

That's when it occurred to me that people's livelihood depended on a solution. I had sixty thousand reasons to contemplate, but only a handful of hours to figure it out.

Unfortunately, the paper thin walls between offices and the fact that I stupidly kept my microphone on allowed my whole staff in on the crisis.

People went into panic mode.

The staff marched into the office and told me that if they didn't get checks by 3:00 p.m. the next day, that they were done working with me.

Mobs are dangerous, and they form quickly.

If that wasn't enough stress, my partnership with Overstock.com was becoming a tenuous one. They were already concerned because I was 45 days behind my deadline airing the first episode of *The Edge*. Realistically, we were still two months away from our debut.

This is not good.

I reassured my staff that this would be taken care of this evening and that everyone would be paid by the next day. They were oddly accepting and appreciative that I was taking this so seriously.

I was convinced I could raise sixty-thousand dollars that night. I just wasn't sure what the plan was. My honesty and intensity calmed everyone down.

Still, the rumblings around the office continued as I called Manuel. It was 7:00 p.m.

"Manuel, can you please come to the office?" I pleaded. "It's urgent."

"Jake, can it wait until tomorrow? I'm eating dinner with..."

"Please," I pleaded.

"Fine, I'm on my way." Manuel said.

I depended on Manuel in the early days. For everything. I always offered him partnership stake in the company and a paycheck, but he politely refused, just reminding me he was enjoying the thrill of the build.

My staff left for the night and wished me good luck. They said that they'd come in the next day, but that they wouldn't work until they had checks.

I fucked this whole thing up.

Brainstorming to save the company

Manuel arrived to find that Maxwell, my childhood friend, and I were the only ones in the office. Together, the three of us, none of who were of legal drinking age, brainstormed ways to raise $60,000 overnight.

"Let's just put all the crazy ideas out there," Manuel suggested.

We agreed. We cracked Red Bulls and stormed bravely into the night.

"Let's get you on CNN and tell your story," Maxwell mentioned.

I called Amy Sabha, an old friend of mine at CNN and left a message. She got back to me ten minutes later. It was too short of notice to book me.

Manuel had another idea.

"What about filming a video and putting it out to your Facebook friends?"

We filmed the video and launched it. It can still be seen online if you search for it.

"What about the tour producer, Max Duncan at Crocs?" I thought.

I called Max Duncan and asked him if he could help with a $100,000 advance to promote Crocs. He said he couldn't, but suggested that I keep on Ford as he got word that they were close to doing the deal with me. That gave me momentarily relief, but it didn't put sixty grand in my bank account.

We wrote down ideas and executed on them as quickly as we came up with them. We didn't think. We just did.

Whatever it takes. Figure this out at any cost.

One of our plans was just to go to the bank the next day and ask for a line of credit.

"I'll just tell them to do it," I blurted out loud.

We put it on the to-do list for the morning.

I was desperate.

Manuel vowed that he would stay all night if needed, but Maxwell had class in the morning.

Manuel and I continued.

One of the ideas we came up with was to call Carrie Barrett in Ireland who loaned me $30,000 already. We thought about asking if she had any more cash she could lend.

It was only 5 a.m. in Ireland and waking her was not a good option. We'd have to wait till early morning in New York before we called.

We discussed calling Ford Motor Company in the morning and see if they'd extend a courtesy check in anticipation of closing my partnership with them.

Asking Overstock.com for an advance despite being months behind our deadline was considered. We were skeptical, but we put it on the list. Nothing was too outlandish.

Neither Manuel nor I slept. I jumped on my trampoline in my office trying to stay awake while he thumbed through his Blackberry.

The night rolled on with no end in sight.

I was weary, but not for a second did I ever consider the possibility of failure that night. I knew it was a matter of time before we figured it out.

The persistence to succeed in those moments of crisis cultivates strength and precision far beyond what we think is possible. The best way to learn how to do this is just to do it. This was the type of real world education I was craving, and despite the anxiousness, I appreciated the lessons, even through the sleepless nights.

My alarm clock rang. 4:00 a.m.—it was time to call Carrie in Dublin. I hoped Carrie would answer.

What was the plan? No plan, just be honest and vulnerable.

"Hello?" Carrie sluggishly answered. It was obvious I woke her up.

"Carrie. Hi, it's Jake," I said. "Do you have a moment?"

"Jake, what in heaven's name is wrong? Isn't it four o'clock in New York?" she asked.

"Well that's just it, Carrie. I'm under a bit of pressure," I said. "I need your help."

"Go on."

"I overdrew my business account yesterday $3,600 and I need to pay my staff today for the past two weeks, and I have no money. I hate to ask you this, but is there any way you might advance me some more money?"

I closed my eyes. Ten seconds of silence felt like eternity.

"How much do you need Jakey? I have other investments I'm looking to make at the moment." Carrie said.

Another deep breath.

"$50,000" I said, sounding like a child who begs for just one more ride at an amusement park.

I needed $60,000, but for some reason, I could only get myself to say fifty. I chickened out and cringed.

"Jake, no. I can't do that. Are you really in that deep?"

Manuel and I sighed in unison.

"Yes," I lamented, rubbing my face. "It's really that deep. Can you do something less? Anything?"

She thought for a moment.

"Yeah, could you do with $10,000?" she asked.

"Thank you, thank you so, so, so much," I acknowledged.

I knew what I was up against and I'd need all the momentum I could get. I gave Carrie my bank account details, and she promised to send the wire that afternoon.

After I disconnected the line, it was 4:17 a.m.

I looked at Manuel. We were both exhausted, but somehow relieved. I realized in that moment I had no truer friend in the world. And I told him.

Manuel and I slept on the floor of my office that night, using garments from the show's wardrobe closet as padding between us and the hardwood floor.

War time

I awoke four hours later, feeling like I was slammed with a ton of bricks. Sasha tip toed in to the office. I squinted. At four foot seven inches, Sasha looked like a monster from where we were on the floor.

"Have you been here all night?" Sasha asked, clearly concerned and trying to figure out what was happening.

"Yeah," I responded, annoyed. "I wasn't kidding when I said I was going to figure this out."

"And did you?" Sasha quipped.

"I'm 20% there," I said.

Sasha looked surprise at my answer.

Manuel woke up. He left to go to class at New York University.

I got down to business.

"Please call our banker at Citibank and tell him I'm coming in for a visit in an hour." I told Sasha.

Sasha grabbed her phone. Her jacket was still on and her purse dangling from her arm.

"Tell him I need a favor, and I'm bringing my TV cameras."

My team started to slowly trickle in. By this point, the staff had grown to more than 25 people.

Pressure's on.

I splashed some water on my face, looked at myself in the mirror and reminded myself that I could this.

Find the money at any cost.

I walked back to my office confident as ever, even though friends told me later I looked like I had aged ten years over night. I called a staff meeting and explained that I understood the position they were taking, and I didn't care if they worked that day or not. I told them that payment would be sorted by afternoon.

I asked a producer to grab two cameras and some microphones and to follow me to Citibank. He agreed. It was 10 a.m.

I decided my best leverage at the bank to get a bridge loan would be to show up with cameras filming. I told them not to stop filming—no matter what happened.

Nothing left to lose.

We walked into the bank, marched passed the front desk and avoided security. I told them I was here for a meeting with Michael Smart, my Citibank business banker, and that he was expecting me.

I took control of an out of control situation. We slithered past and entered the banker's office before getting caught. Michael motioned to security that I wasn't a threat.

It was 10:08, and I had a 3:00 p.m. deadline to find this money. I needed fifty-thousand more dollars. I had no time to fuck around.

"Michael," I greeted my banker with a big smile. "So nice to see you."

"Jake, you really can't be doing this. What's going on here?"

"Never-you-mind, Michael, all is well," I said, quickly changing the subject. "I have a favor to ask you and it's, well, it's a bit uncomfortable."

Michael was apprehensive. He wanted the cameras out. I ignored him.

"As you know, we have a great relationship with Citibank."

I took a deep breath.

Was I really this crazy? This was as close to holding up a bank as I'd ever get.

My hunger to win and remain in the game was greater than anything else in my life. I tried to disguise it as a young twenty-something entrepreneur with a big dream. But, you can't *really* disguise this level of insanity.

My adrenaline pumped and I was as high as a kite.

"I've gotten myself into a bit of a pickle," I explained. "I don't expect you to get me out of it. I'll get myself out of it."

Michael looked confused. It was a hostage situation. And I wasn't holding back.

"What I need from you is a commitment that you will not bounce any checks that are cashed today at Citibank," I said.

I didn't want to out rightly ask for cash, because I knew I wouldn't be approved for a line of credit and that it would take more time than I had.

However, I thought that asking for an off-the-record commitment from the bank to not bounce any checks was a good solution.

It was essentially an emergency line of credit without calling it as such.

Michael smirked. He knew precisely what I was doing. He already signed a TV appearance release form weeks prior so I could legally use any footage that I was taking now.

I knew Michael was in line for a promotion and he certainly didn't want to appear like the bad guy crushing a kid's dreams. It wouldn't be good for business or his promotion. Plus, it would be good TV.

Remember what I was saying earlier about knowing the perception of what you want to create, and to market the perception first, before creating it? I used what I had at my disposal: a TV release form signed weeks before, a somewhat frayed relationship with my banker, and a camera and a microphone.

I wasn't going to actually use the footage from that day. I just wanted to create the perception that I might. No one was the wiser, and if I was arrested, that'd make the segment even better.

It was manipulative and deceitful, but I had to find this money. I also knew with total certainty that we'd pay it all back. I just needed a lifeline. The alternative was my production completely shutting down.

And if we shut down it would kill all momentum and all of the deals in the pipeline (including my Ford deal). I couldn't afford that loss. I couldn't afford not to pay my team. I couldn't afford to fail.

I was stuck between a rock and a hard place. The moment I stepped into Michael's office, he was as stuck as I was. He knew he had to do something. In less than five minutes I ruined his morning. And he let me know it.

"Well, Jake, I just don't know, I mean, I need to call corporate and see if we can..."

"Friend," I interjected, at the risk of sounding condescending. "I've stayed up all night and my staff has threatened to quit if they can't cash their checks at your institution this afternoon. I just need your commitment to see this through with me."

"I'll call your cell in twenty minutes," he replied. "Now could you please get out of my office?"

Though I didn't leave with a commitment, I felt we were slowly cracking the code.

Moments later, as I was walking back to my office, my phone rang.

"We won't bounce any checks that are cashed today," Michael from Citibank assured me. "Up to $25,000, that's it."

My shoulders relaxed and I felt relief.

"It's a pleasure doing business with you as always, sir," I said. "I appreciate it." I truly did.

And just like that, two of the ideas that Manuel and I brainstormed at midnight worked. We were half way to 60K, and it wasn't even lunchtime.

Anything is possible.

Feeling buzzed from the recent surge of successes, I decided I'd go 3-for-3.

"Sasha, please get me Jen Wells at Ford on the line."

Jen Wells is the senior director for Ford's advertising agency, JWT Detroit. The role of an advertising agency is to vet and determine which opportunities are presented to the client (in this case, Ford). It's a complex series of evaluations, both creative and mathematical, to determine if a client like Ford wants to do business with a guy like me.

JWT was like a large gatekeeper for Ford.

Last we spoke, Ford said they needed more time.

"Jen, it's Jake," I said, sounding upbeat

"Jake! How are you?" Jen asked.

I didn't let on to what we were going through, as I didn't have a deal signed yet with Ford. The cameras rolled as I talked with Jen. I tried to temper my exhaustion but I wonder if I came across as manic instead.

"I'm doing great, thanks! A pretty bouncy day here in New York," I said, referring to the possibility of bouncing some checks.

Sasha laughed.

"Listen, Jen. I'm stretching a few things right now financially and I'd really like to be able to take advantage of some opportunities," I said. "I was hoping I could get the Ford commitment today."

"I can't make a commitment today," Jen said regretfully. "The client is still reviewing your documents, and I'm confident it will be yours, but I can't confirm it for you."

"No problem, Jenny. I really appreciate it," I said before ending the call. "I can't wait to meet you for a drink in Detroit once we get this wrapped up."

I was thrilled. This was just the confidence booster I needed.

If I can see my company through the storm today, Ford will be mine tomorrow.

I hung up. And just then, I had *another* idea.

Give away when you have nothing left

"Sasha, go get Brian and the few others who have decided to actually work today, I'm bringing you guys to lunch."

A universal teaching that many of my spiritual and business gurus have shared is that in times of need, one must give. I had no money left, but I knew that going to lunch would be great for everyone. It would also confuse them, and bring a light-hearted reminder that we're supposed to be having fun at work.

We went to our regular joint, a café on Beach Street in TriBeCa. Even though I was so close to losing everything, it gave me a huge relief to treat my team to lunch. My shoulders relaxed. We laughed about the ridiculousness of the situation we were in. We ate a ton of food. And I used the last few dollars I had to pay the bill.

I talk about the feeling of relief often. For me, it's a personal guidance system and a wonderful indicator if I'm on the right track. If I don't feel relief, I re-evaluate what I can do to change my circumstance.

Following your instinct

It was 1 p.m. when we returned from lunch. I nervously clapped my hands together to wake myself up. My senior team was in my office, including Brian, Sasha, Peter and Lori.

I quietly announced that I'd call Overstock.com and ask them for an advance of cash. I couldn't see any other option.

One of the executive producers, Peter, firmly protested my decision, suggesting it would be relationship suicide.

"Homicide or suicide?" I asked. "Either way, the ship is sinking and I'm out of options." I said.

Peter argued his point before I cut him off...

"I believe that if I'm honest with Overstock.com, if I tell them what's going on, it'll strengthen my relationship with them instead of ruining it," I said.

He wasn't convinced.

I had to follow my intuition. I had a team around me that had many more years of experience than me, but they didn't have much at stake. I had my reputation on the line and it was my name on the company and all the checks and agreements. I had people's families in mind.

All too often, we give up what we believe is right because someone else is louder or more persistent in their opinion.

For example, even though the situation that day was stressful, and I was exhausted and unsure of the future, when I considered calling Overstock. com for the advance, I physically felt relief. I felt good thinking about my connection with Stormy Simon, the chief marketing officer, and Nicole, her right hand. I felt this call would strengthen the relationship, not ruin it.

Feeling good is my indicator when a decision is the right one.

If something's not working, leave it be, move on to something else, and circle back when it feels better. This is so simple, and I see people try so hard to make something feel good that doesn't. All you have to do is leave it for another day. And recognizing that sometimes you'll simply have to…

8

LOSE THE BATTLE TO WIN THE WAR

Accepting Casualties and Honor
Those Who Fight by Your Side

All war represents a failure of diplomacy.

— Tony Benn

Overstock.com's contribution to *The Edge* was $59,000 to date.

I was months late on the delivery of their first episode, but explained to them that it was because of our campus music tour. Under the agreement, they'd pay us monthly installments for the remainder of the $125,000 commitment.

Just as I was about to pick up the phone to call Overstock, I heard a knock at my door. It was my head writer, Katie Bashinelli.

She approached my desk.

"Jake," she whispered. "I'm so sorry; I just can't do this anymore. It's too bumpy for me. I can't work like this. I have to leave, I'm done."

I was shocked.

"But, but... Katie, I'm just about to...wait..."

"No, I can't. It's not healthy for me."

There was no talking her out of it. She was quitting. She lost hope. I thanked her for her work and told her we'd pay what we owed her just as soon as I could. I gave her a big hug.

"You see," I said to Peter who encouraged me not to call Overstock. com, waving to my departing head writer. "What the fuck do you propose we do to stop what's about to happen?"

He was silent.

Isolating fear as quickly as possible

If hopelessness and fear continued to spread among my staff, I'd lose my whole team. Losing people who've gotten to know me and my style and who made up the individual parts of a complex machine could be almost as detrimental to my organization as not having any money at all. I was in the middle of an all-out assault to keep my company—and my dream–alive.

This was war.

"I'm calling Overstock," I announced to Peter. "Be positive and sup-portive please."

Nicole Bondoc, advertising director for Overstock.com, answered on the second ring. We had a conversation and I explained my situation thor-oughly. I told her I needed an advance check of $30,000. The call could have made her an adversary; I wanted her to become even more of an ally.

Nicole gasped on the phone.

That didn't sound good.

She was on speakerphone, so it didn't reassure my senior team either.

"Nicole," I said, "I need to know that you can do this by 3:00 p.m., otherwise the production shuts down."

Nicole said she would look into it.

I hung up the phone and began my silent wait for Nicole's answer. It was 2:15 p.m.

The mass exodus of my once thriving staff continued at 2:30p.m.

Two writers, Jim and Sally, who were famous around the offices of *The Onion*, walked into my office and explained that they couldn't continue working either. They were married, and were hired by Katie, so it was clear that fear was becoming toxic. I was losing my footing and leverage.

Well, at least the payroll would be easier to meet the following week

Greg, one of my best producers who cut his teeth at MTV, also quit.

I wished them well and meant it.

Just then, I emailed Nicole Bondoc at Overstock.com, desperate.

> Subject: Free Brownies.
> November 9, 2007
> 2:37 p.m.
> "Hey Nicole, Just wanted to thank you for considering this. I know it's a lot to ask for. No matter what, I'll make this up to you. Free brownies at the minimum.
> Love, Jake."

I went to grab some water and wash my face.

When I returned back into my office, I asked if anything new had come in. Someone at my desk said I had an email from Overstock.com about free brownies.

I ran to my desk and opened the email.

> Subject: Re: Free Brownies
> November 9, 2007
> 2:55 p.m.
> "Send me the brownies, and I'll send you a check for $30,000.
> Love, Nicole."

I called Nicole back to see if this was true.

She said yes and I cried.

The entire office erupted with cheers and laughter. Against all odds, we raised the last $30,000 from Overstock.com, five minutes before our deadline.

$10,000 from Carrie in Ireland
$25,000 emergency line of credit from Citibank
$30,000 from Overstock.com

We raised $65,000 overnight.
Without sleep.
Without any Hollywood connections.
Without rich parents.
I called Manuel.

"Manuel, we did it," I screamed. "It worked. The plan worked! Overstock.com just committed the last $30,000."

He laughed. I bounced off the walls.

"Congratulations." Manuel said to me. He sounded as exhausted as me.

Together, Manuel and I brainstormed and executed a plan to save the company. This was a major victory for me then and one that still excites me today.

I lost half my staff that day. I pressed on nonetheless and remain singularly focused. I enlisted the help of allies and empowered them. I prayed and tried to remain positive. I gave gratitude to folks at lunch and I learned that if I hadn't followed my instinct and dared to call Overstock.com, I may not have survived to write about it. At the very least, the story would've been much shorter.

But for now, I had every reason to celebrate. In fact, I counted...

9

100,000 REASONS TO CELEBRATE IN LONDON

Get Out of the Office, Meet People and Expect Greatness from Everybody and Greatness You Shall Receive (Not to Mention Some Cash!)

There are only two ways to live your life. One is as though nothing is a miracle. The other is as though everything is a miracle.

— ALBERT EINSTEIN

I learned the importance of keeping my eyes on the books after I had to raise $60,000 in 21 hours. What I failed to learn is that even in the face of losing everything I *still* didn't hire a damn accountant.

Just because my finances aren't flourishing doesn't mean I can turn a blind eye to them and hope the status magically improves.

I'll admit that in the early days I thought things would magically work out if I believed they would. It's why *The Secret* isn't totally effective. It teaches to "think and so it shall be," which is a great starting point, but there's much more to the spiritual laws of manifesting, including detachment and gratitude.

Another thing struck me post-financial crisis. Why in the world did I feel justified spending $15,000 a week in staffing costs? It was inappropriate. I should've found a way to shrink that number by half, even if it meant letting go of people I loved.

Ignorance is bliss.

After the fiasco, I decided to spend Thanksgiving in London. I had a very dear friend there—Susie Pearl—and she agreed to host me and even cook an American Thanksgiving dinner for laughs.

Surrounding yourself with greatness

Susie Pearl was a brilliant PR wonder woman who built her PR firm into a multi-million dollar success. She used to roll with Madonna and Michael Jackson, and launched the Spice Girls. She rocked the MTV Europe Music Awards and led her team in the 90s and 00s to many big business successes. Those days are long gone. She since sold her business and now prefers the quieter life of writing and raising her young son.

Always willing to offer me prophetic jewels on how to run my business effectively, which often led to personal breakthroughs, Susie Pearl also taught me how to broker deals in the entertainment industry. She was a true ally in my early days. She taught me the spiritual side of business, and how that was equally important to being the risk-taking, aggressive dealmaker that I was becoming.

On the Friday afternoon before my staff left for Thanksgiving break, Lori Fitch, my executive producer and the woman in charge of the day-to-day of my finances, came into my office.

"Now Jake," she began in a tone I knew all too well. "You know that when you come back from London you have $49,500 due to the staff, right?" Lori said, holding eye contact to make sure that I heard her.

"Yes, Lor," I responded casually.

"Yeah, and you have to pay some of the company credit cards," Lori reminded me, which we had to free up in order to make petty cash available.

How the hell am I going to raise $50,000? And on Thanksgiving week?
Lori left the office.

The entertainment industry shuts down the third week of November and Ford hasn't given me a commitment yet.

I was deeply concerned, just for a moment, but decided to let it go. I trusted something would happen.

Sweet denial.

Susie Pearl called me from London as I was boarding my flight that night. As usual, she wasted no time sharing her excitement.

"Jaaakeyyyyy!" she screamed. "We are so happy to have you here, lovey!"

"Me too, Susie," I said. "I really needed to take this week off."

"So listen Jake, I have a friend I want you to meet while you're here," she said. "He is really interested in your ideas with your non-profit foundation and he's curious about *The Edge.*"

It sounded like Susie had something up her sleeve (she usually did) but I couldn't put my finger on it.

"I think it will be very good for you guys to meet."

"No problem. Sounds great," I told her. "My flight is boarding, got to jet."

As I was about to hang up, Susie interrupted.

"One other thing, Jakey boy," she said. "Just so you know he's one of the richest men I know."

She giggled like a schoolgirl and hung up before I could respond.

A hard lesson on human capital

Human capital is a crucial element in running a business. Even those who don't receive a paycheck from you can turn out to be some of your most important investments. Treat them well.

I leaned on Susie Pearl for many years, and until recently I had failed to recognize that I took from her much more than I gave. We had lots of laughter and love in our friendship. But I took a lot. My taking came in the form of desperate 2 a.m. manic calls for help or guidance, trips to stay at her estate in England, accompanying her to the island of Mallorca off the coast of Spain for summer getaways, and a consistent attitude of "me first." It was fine at the beginning, in fact Susie Pearl loved it, but over time, my selfishness took over and left nothing more in the relationship for her to give.

This is Susie and me hanging out at a villa in Mallorca, an island off the coast of Spain. This woman changed my life forever, and caused more belly aching laughter than one should have in a lifetime.

A London Thanksgiving

I arrived at Susie Pearl's townhouse the next morning. It rested on the south end of the River Thames, a three-story million dollar home in the highly fashionable Chiswick area of London. I claimed the guesthouse in the garden immediately.

Susie and I hopped in a cab on Thanksgiving Day to meet Oli and Sarah. I had no clue what to expect. Susie told me Oli and Sarah were billionaire Canadians who she recently started hanging out with. They were both intrigued by my story.

We ended up in the Kensington section of London at a swanky sushi joint called Zuma. Susie Pearl's friends hadn't yet arrived. Zuma's loud electronic music pulsated and felt more like a club scene in Ibiza than it did a Thanksgiving afternoon in London.

"What does Oli want to talk to me about, Susie?" I asked over my first sip of green tea.

"Think of it as if you're meeting two new friends." Susie Pearl said.

She had a glimmer in her eye. Before I could investigate I felt someone patting me on my shoulder. I turned around to see a plump, graying man wearing a dark suit.

"Hi Oli, it's nice to finally meet you," I said.

"Jake, a pleasure," Oli said.

Susie stood up to hug Oli's wife, Sarah. I extended my arm after they released. We all sat down and ordered sushi.

As Sarah and Susie caught up, Oli focused on me. Our conversation circled into non-profits and my desire to elevate education in the world. I talked about how important I thought it was to teach students in poorer countries the basics of math and science but equally how important it was to teach spirituality. Oli agreed, and the conversation sped up.

All at once, Oli made a sharp right turn. The energy shifted with it.

"So tell me about your business," he said.

"Well, you know, it's a production company and we are producing a TV show called *The Edge*," I said. "Our social media campaign called 'Jake after Jimmy' was rather successful."

"Interesting," Oli said.

I explained how Jake after Jimmy was driving tens of thousands of young people to engage and say they "wanted their Jake after Jimmy." He was intrigued, and we shared a laugh.

"You must go through a lot of money to do all that, especially by yourself with no funding support."

"I go through a lot of money each week," I said, somewhat proudly. "My burn rate is pretty high."

"Well, that must be really challenging," Oli said.

I became curious about his questioning, and didn't understand where it was headed.

"What would it mean to you to be able to level off your cash flow challenge?"

I had to think about it for a moment.

"It would mean everything!" I said, "That's the whole point, stabilize and grow, and then sell or get acquired."

I wanted so much for *The Edge* to have thirteen successful episodes after *Jimmy Kimmel Live* and get picked up by a network for season two.

"I would like to help you," Oli said. "Let me give you some money."

I stopped chewing.

The energy just got weirder.

"Oh," I said. "You want to help me?"

While my new benefactor tried to figure out my reaction, Susie Pearl kicked me under the table. Hard.

This guy wasn't just going to give me money, was he? And for what?

Receiving money from the other side of the Atlantic was nothing new for me. Carrie had done the same thing just months before. But that was different. I was friends with her son and I had known her for a while before she gave me the thirty grand.

I scoffed at the offer.

"I like you, Oli, but I can't afford the emotional investment of discussing a partnership with you," I said matter-of-factly.

Oli ignored my childish behavior.

"What is your monthly burn rate?" he asked.

"About $100,000," I over-estimated just for fun.

He continued without skipping a beat.

"Fine then, why don't I transfer you $100,000 next week? No paperwork, no investments," he offered.

What the fuck just happened?

"Pay it back when you can and I'll pay it forward, and if you can't pay it back, that's fine too."

As I considered my bills back in New York (totaling $49,500 by the time I arrived the following Monday), my eyes welled with emotion.

By now, Susie Pearl, Sarah and Oli were all smiling at me. It felt like I was in another universe. Certainly this couldn't be my *real* life.

"I just, I just don't know what to say," I said. "Excuse, me. I have to use the restroom."

It's a mind game. With ourselves.

Human consciousness is extremely powerful. The ability to influence yourself allows you to influence others. Influencing yourself is also known as leverage. Getting leverage on yourself requires consistent and deliberate awareness of your thoughts, feelings and emotions, and directing them in a direction that brings you relief and joy, from only that place should you take action to get things done.

It's not easy to shift your reality. But it is simple. The conversations we have with ourselves are usually on auto-pilot. Turn off the auto-pilot. Get deliberate. If you want a different output result from your computer, you'd probably consider inputting something different, until you got the desired result, right? The same is true with leverage on your mind.

I assured myself over and over again that I would find the money needed during my week in London. I didn't know how and I didn't obsess about it. I just acted in accordance with the belief system that I would find it and that I would be okay either way.

Imagine if I had let the "what-if's" of owing my team money paralyze me or impact my trip. I would never have gotten on the plane, and never met Oli.

So even if I hadn't found the $100,000 in London at Thanksgiving dinner, my emotional baseline was set so that I'd be okay either way. You'll be okay either way. What if your belief system included that whatever happens, you're OK? Would you take more chances?

With or without the money, I'd be okay.

To the outside world, I am a freewheeling youngster with big dreams, big balls, big hair and a big mouth. People consider me extremely lucky. I'm simply running my mind so that whatever happens in my life, I am able to find relief. That's it. That's the trick. Lucky me.

I had spent months and months self-examining and shifting old belief systems when that moment in November 2007 happened with Oli, Susie Pearl and Sarah in London. In a sense, I was prepared for the luck I was experiencing.

Again, I was okay with that money or without it. For those who say: "You wouldn't be shouting about your success and luck if Oli hadn't given the money to you" I respond: "You are absolutely right. I only talk about what feels good to talk about."

People say to me "that's too good to be true." I never understood that saying anyways. I say...

10

WHEN THINGS GET TOO GOOD TO BE TRUE, LET THE GOOD TIMES ROLL

Private Islands, Spiritual Retreats (and a Very Concerned Staff)

As I make my slow pilgrimage through the world, a certain sense of beautiful mystery seems to gather and grow.

— A.C. Benson

I returned to New York the Sunday after Thanksgiving.

I called my executive producers in for a meeting and told them they'd never believe what happened to me while in London. Of course, they couldn't even fathom. Lori Fitch said she wouldn't believe it till he saw the bank statement.

Four days later, with an overdrawn bank account of $150 (I bounced a rent check), the $100,000 from my Thanksgiving power lunch in London showed up in my account, in full.

Saying YES

That Friday, my phone rang and Sarah's name showed up. She and Oli were both eager to confirm that I received the money.

"Listen, I'm in South Africa right now, but I feel like our work isn't quite done." Sarah said to me.

What? Your husband gives me a hundred grand and now you want to talk about?

I waited for the shoe to drop.

"I'm flying to the west coast of Canada to our private island retreat next week," she said. "I wondered if you'd like to come out and visit me for the weekend. I didn't really get a chance to get to know you in London."

I was shocked, but enthusiastically accepted the offer. My assistant Sasha, eavesdropping, giggled.

It's evident that between the $100,000 showing up in my account and my escapades to western Canada a few days later, my staff not only respected me, but they were getting more curious about how exactly all of this was happening.

The staff wondered if I was having an affair or if I was being manipulated or used for the money. I rejected each point vehemently.

How dare they suggest such a thing?

The following weekend, I flew to Vancouver and took a private seaplane to Sarah's island. It was a brisk Fall day.

The home was a modern masterpiece. The most noted part was the automatic glass garage door that opened up and exposed the living room to the ocean, overlooking the mountain tops. Whales were just off the coast. I walked around the property the first day I arrived, in awe.

Sarah was a lovely petite woman, soft speaking, and she was gracious, healthy and vibrant host. After an afternoon steam bath, I went to my private cabin on the estate and checked in with my staff back in New York. Everyone was still working. I told them all is well.

That evening, Sarah prepared a vegetable soup. We ate it, in silence. It was awkward and relieving all at once. I never ate with someone in silence before. I learned how to that weekend.

A truly unbelievable set of events was unfolding.

The weekend flew by and I returned to New York with a curious staff and an even more curious family. I downplayed the experience to a simple weekend with a friend. This, of course, infuriated them as my pop-culture obsessed team wanted the gossipy details. We didn't have time for details, because I was too excited about what good stuff might happen next. I was ready for...

11

THE FORD FIASCO, FEATURING TV'S JAKE SASSEVILLE

Why Ford Gave Me a Car, a Payday and a Reason to Hate my 1989 Pontiac Grand Am

Take all the fools out of this world and there wouldn't be any fun living in it, or profit.

— Josh Billings

It was the Monday morning after my British Columbia getaway. The visions of whales serenely swimming in the ocean quickly faded into another type of whale in the heart of Manhattan

My direct line buzzed.

I was busy preparing for an important show taping later that day. I let Sasha take it.

"Jake," Sasha said, poking her head in the door. "It's Jen Wells from Ford calling."

Oh shit. I wonder if this is THE call.

Jen and her team at JWT Detroit were evaluating our $275,000 proposal to Ford Motor Company for months. I pitched Jen weekly since September. It was now December.

My eager phone manner masked my nervousness.

We did the usual tango —pleasantries before business.

"So," Jen began. "We reviewed your proposal and appreciate all of the hard work you and your team have put in..."

Fuck. Just tell me goddamnit. Are you in or not?

"...as you know, we presented it to the Ford client here in Detroit for a decision..."

Please just say yes. Shit. This totally sounds like a pass.

"...and, we all think this would be a great fit," Jen said.

"So you're...in?" I choked.

"We're in, Jake," Jen replied assumingly. "We're with you."

I jumped up and down. I kissed my assistant Sasha. I even ran down the hall in my office with Jen still on the phone, screaming about my newest advertiser.

"Ford is in!" I exclaimed until it echoed through the office.

$275,000.

Money was indeed flowing.

Could this get any better?

My heart raced.

"Jen, I can't thank you enough. You fucking rock."

"It's our pleasure," Jen said. "We review a lot of proposals and consider a lot of opportunities, so unfortunately, we often have to say no."

"Thank you for not saying no," I said.

"You and your team are invited to come and meet us in Detroit next week to go over details." Jen offered.

"Oh we'll be there, Jenny," I said. "As long as I can bring cameras into the room."

After some hesitation, I convinced Jen to say yes to cameras in the room.

Authenticity gives you power

Jen understood the game I was playing. She understood the level of transparency and authenticity I created with my brand gave me a competitive edge. She was a true renegade marketer, working for a massive company but still keeping her work relevant. She was, after all, in charge of innovative marketing and relationships for Ford.

It is unheard of for a company like Ford to ever let cameras into a closed-door meeting. The magic of what we were creating (indeed, what we stood for) resonated with people so much that rules were bent.

"One other thing, Jake." Jen interrupted.

I was silent.

"We need to discuss payment terms," Jen suggested. "It's Ford's policy to not pay anything up front for a deal like this."

Fuck there's a catch.

"But, we understand that in your situation, we'll need to be flexible," Jen said.

Thank God, some money up front.

"But we also need your help with something," Jen said, imploring my assistance.

The back and forth was dizzying. I held my breath on every word.

Jen told me that because they needed to spend Ford's money before the end of the year (it was December already), they'd need me to accept the whole check up front.

The whole check? At once?

This had never happened before—ever.

"Um, sure?" I stammered. "What's the catch for me?"

New rules were being written daily.

"The only catch is that you'll have to also accept your new 2008 Ford Focus in December as well," Jen said.

"I get a new car, excuse me?"

Jen giggled.

"Yes, of course, you'll pick up the new car at the dealership next week."

I fell to the floor. Sasha thought I fainted. I was overwhelmed. The last several weeks of my life amounted to be one hell of a roller coaster ride. I couldn't say anything else to Jen.

What a dream come true.

I get a car. I get the cash. My show is saved (again). And Ford was going to allow cameras into the meeting! In some strange way, this surge of successes legitimized the challenges we experienced to get here. In eight years, not one network gave me a green light. Suddenly, within three months of deciding I'd create my own path to late night TV stardom, I had industry leaders behind me and had generated $570,000 in capital.

The best part: Jen Wells called to share the news on my 21st birthday.

I thanked Jen and hung up.

I phoned my publicist immediately to release the news.

21-Year-Old Late Night Talk Show Host Jake Sasseville Nabs Ford as Second National Advertiser for New Show Airing After *Jimmy Kimmel Live*

I was learning how to be a master megaphone and left no stone unturned. I felt like the stars were aligning.

Success and failure are (almost) indistinguishable

The line between success and failure is so thin. You might think about giving up when times are tough, but truly, the difference between getting a call from Ford and my company almost folding three weeks prior is an example of how thin the line between success and failure is.

The YES you need is sometimes right around the corner.

My staying power is part-resiliency that I've built up, part-determination, part-delusional thinking and part-luck. The truth is, I'm successful because I've chosen to be successful. I've had advertising executives tell me that part of the reason they've stuck with me and invested in me over the years is because I don't run away when things get bad and I stay in the game.

They trust me because even though I'm occasionally reckless, I'm consistent. Powerful decision makers recognize winners, and sometimes winners are born out of the ashes of part-time failure.

My failures weren't my focus. Success was. I was ready to meet Jen Wells and the executives…

12

ON FORD'S HOME TURF

... And Why I Hired a Jobless Detroit Autoworker as my Chauffeur.

My life has been one great big joke, a dance that's walked a song that's spoke, I laugh so hard I almost choke when I think about myself.

— MAYA ANGELOU

We traveled to Detroit to meet the Ford Motor Company executives. I traveled with my producer, director and cameraman.

I had no clue what to expect but we were all very excited.

Disrupt the system. Every system.

I called Jen a day before arriving and asked if she could send a car to the airport. She said she couldn't, and that we'd have to take a cab or rent a car.

The fourth biggest car company in the world couldn't send me and my team a car service? Really?

Then, a light-bulb moment.

I'm a sucker for turning a problem into an opportunity. I love an opportunity that I can turn into a press story.

I asked Sasha to go online and search for unemployed Detroit autoworkers.

"Search on Craigslist or something," I said to Sasha when she looked confused at my assignment. "Find me someone who's out of work and who wants to play chauffeur for a day."

I thought it'd be fun to hire someone out of work to drive us around Detroit, and film it as part of the show.

Sasha figured it out.

She found a married man named Dan, father of two, who just lost his job. We offered a $100 stipend.

Turned out our new driver Dan was even more excited than we were. He and his entire family met us at Detroit Metro Airport.

Dan's kids created a poster board the night before. It read: WELCOME TO THE D, JAKE!

As we rattled down Interstate 94 toward Ford headquarters, I was squished in the backseat between the producer and the director. My cameraman shot the whole thing from the front.

Dan alerted us that his house was on the way to Ford, suggesting that we stop by.

"Sure," I said, hesitantly. "We have a few hours to kill."

Dan was proud of his family and his home.

We were in a 1992 GMC that seemed to have trouble getting past sixty-miles-per-hour on the interstate. It was subtle comedy, but raw and real. We shot everything and included it in the show. I liked infusing my show with doses of real people and real events. It made the hyper-reality of everything else in my life feel balanced.

Escalate levels of absurdity to appeal to the masses

"Dan, I was thinking," I said, as we drove to Ford. "We'd like your help with something."

"Anything Jake, whatcha need?" Dan enthusiastically volunteered.

"Well, we have a camera guy here with us, but we don't have anyone to hold our boom microphone pole," I explained. "Do you have anything to do while we're at the meeting?"

Dan said that he planned to wait in the car.

Perfect.

"Join us in the meeting, and would you hold our boom pole for us?"

Dan agreed.

A boom pole is a long stick with a big microphone on the end of it. It's held delicately over the head of the person speaking to catch sound. It's a physically intense job since you have to hold the heavy boom pole over your head for hours.

We arrived on the seventh floor at the Ford compound and waited for Jen Wells. I was dressed even more casual than usual – a red graphic tee with a half-naked woman on it covered by a sharp black blazer. Everyone else had on jeans and t-shirts.

Dan, Detroit's newest boom pole operator, stood out like a sore thumb, a rotund 400-pound man with an unshaven face and holes in his jeans. Not the cool, trendy holes either.

The juxtapositions were awkward and brilliantly perfect. Most business people might make sure their presentation or dress code was air tight before the biggest meeting of their lives. Not me.

"Jen!" I screamed, running up for a hug. She was with other Ford execs.

I introduced everybody and turned to my unemployed-autoworker-turned-chauffeur-turned-boom-operator.

Without hesitation and as cameras rolled, I called Ford out.

"I couldn't believe when Ford wouldn't send me a car, Jen," I said to her. "So we went on Craigslist and did some virtual hitchhiking."

Jen looked confused, but shook Dan's hand anyway.

"This is Dan, he's chauffeuring us around since you couldn't afford to," I said. "And turns out he's always wanted to hold a microphone."

The Ford executives didn't know if this was real or fake. That's what made it so funny. They went along with it, and we did too. We played it as if it was real, because it was.

Ten minutes into the meeting at Ford, Dan *fell asleep,* slamming the microphone (ten pounds) onto the Ford executive's head from above, causing a shriek and a pound. The room jolted.

Ouch. The price of unscripted comedy.

It's amazing these people (or anyone for that matter) gave me money.

Indeed, we were bringing a new level of vulnerability to late night TV.

As the meeting wrapped up, I asked Ford why in the world they chose me to do business with me.

Because you're not Craig Ferguson

They said that they had considered other late night alternatives, but felt that we would best reach the late night audience, even though our viewership would be far less than Craig Ferguson or Jimmy Kimmel.

I believe it was this willingness to be totally raw with our audience (and our partners) that caused us to be so successful in our early days. People 'got us' because they could identify and see a piece of themselves in each of us. That's why I put my staff on camera. We were full of young, hungry 20-somethings trying to make it in New York City.

Having Dan hold our microphone (and fall asleep in the meeting) was real and unrehearsed. It made us more likeable, not less. It made for great television and showed we didn't know what the hell we were doing. We embraced our shortcomings. Out loud and without apology.

> *"The more real you get, the more unreal the world gets."*
>
> — JOHN LENNON

Someone interrupted the meeting from outside the door.

"I didn't want to interrupt for very long," the man, unknown to me at that point, said. "But I wanted to meet you, Jake."

Turns out he was Kurt Ehrle, an EVP of Finance at JWT Detroit. He had personally signed off on the deal a week prior.

"We've put our asses on the line for this, Jake," Kurt said frankly. "And we fully expect you to do a terrific job."

He paused, almost for effect. "Because we can't afford for this not to work. Do we understand each other?"

Suddenly, shit got real. I became nervous but concealed it with congeniality.

I thanked Kurt and assured him we'd make him proud on his leap of faith.

Words I'd regret very shortly.

I got back to New York and started editing *The Edge with Jake Sasseville*. When I started to watch what we created, I don't think I realized the controlled chaos and cultural nuances the show stood for. We had everything from...

13

CAST MEMBERS FROM "30 ROCK," GUY FROM MAINE, PIMPS, WHORES AND OTHER FIRST SEASON GUESTS AND SHENANIGANS

Despite the challenges, The Edge was radically different than the rest

Impossible is a word only to be found in the dictionary of fools.

— NAPOLEAN BONAPARTE

I think that, creatively, *The Edge* spoke to the hopes, dreams and curiosities of my generation. It was aspirational as it showed a young staff teeming away at creating television. We thought of *The Edge* as a reality-talk show from the point of view of a young 21-year-old, and how exactly he goes from dreaming of late night fame to actually creating it.

In between "regular" late night segments and sketches, we turned the camera on ourselves and crafted a narrative that was as entertaining as it was raw. People on my team had their own storylines and were genuinely funny. It humanized the show and made it more about our audience than just about me. I loved that.

We never had much time to pre-create, so we were often left to come up with ideas a few days before, and make up stuff on the spot when we filmed. I always pushed my team to fill a segment with plenty of variables. I knew that if we had variables, my writing and producing team could play around and create brilliance.

For example, "Jake goes to interview a nude model" turned into "Jake goes to interview a nude model, and he himself gets nude for the drawing session" turned into "Jake interviews a nude model, while nude himself, and he calls his mother to tell her what he's doing for his birthday."

After my writing staff quit, I hired two of the funniest people I'd ever worked with, James and Sal. Both guys had known each other for fifteen years and were part of a comedy improv troupe called "The Tenderloins." Rightfully so, Sal, James and the two other guys with "The Tenderloins" pitched and won a development deal for their own show on TruTV called "Impractical Jokers," which just got green lit for a second season. I'm honored to have worked with them early on.

Going to work was like plunging off a bridge with the same group of people every day, except the water seemed further and further and the bungee cord was longer and longer. The fall seemed to be never-ending. As a child, I imagined that this is what my life would be like, but I never knew how much fucking fun I'd have doing it.

Dunkin' Donuts as the "unofficial studio" of The Edge

When we got a deal with Dunkin' Donuts, we chose to book some celebrities. We decided to go with cast members from one of our favorite shows, NBC's *30 Rock*. One of them, who played Tina Fey's assistant Cerie, was a cute, young blond named Katrina Bowden. We told them the "TV studio" was actually a 24/7 Dunkin' Donuts on 23rd Street in Manhattan. Dunkin' Donuts became our unofficial studio.

We thought it was cheeky and innovative.

But we knew that just having Katrina from *30 Rock* as a guest wouldn't be enough.

I had found an a capella group who sang every day on the New York City subway system. Despite the fact that none of these guys had a cell phone (or a real working number), my producers worked miracles and got them to *also* show up at our Dunkin' Donuts "studio."

As we continued to layer the segment, someone blurted out: "munchkin tossing competition." I chimed in and said that Katrina and I should toss the munchkins into each other's mouths. At first, Katrina's team said NO, but after a little back and forth, the publicist went for it.

A few days later, Katrina arrived and looked stunning. Dunkin' execs made sure we had nice shots of the store. The store remained open while we filmed, creating an odd voyeuristic sensation for Dunkin' guests and *The Edge* team. We were both in each other's worlds.

A view of our 'unofficial' studio set-up at a Dunkin Donuts. It was ridiculous, but somehow it worked.

As we broke for commercial, the a capella group was cued to sing an old doo-whoop song. They were, however, arguing with a producer to be paid up front as we went to commercial. Cameras caught it all, and when they realized they were on TV, they went from argument to song without missing a beat.

Two minutes later, back from commercial, the a capella group sang an original tune called "Jake after Jimmy." Katrina laughed at the mayhem. I loved being ringleader to the circus.

Over the next several weeks, AdAge, The Observer and New York Magazine led with stories that applauded our over-the-top mockery of product placement and seamless partnership with Dunkin' Donuts.

Casey Corrigan was the PR executive for Dunkin Donuts, and in this photo she's clearly making sure that I understand *not* to go over the line with Dunkin.

Maine Man

A few days later I had the idea that, since I was from Maine, and Mainers were known for being eccentric, quirky, quiet and hermit-like, that we'd do an open-call casting for the "Mainiest Mainer" to showcase the stereotype. The winner would receive a trip to New York City and a day on *The Edge* with me. People couldn't tell if I was making fun of my home state, or honoring it. That was the point.

After we promoted the "competition" all over the State of Maine and received a handful of interested people, we found Gary Libby, a stoic 26-year veteran fisherman of the lonely Maine seas. Every winter, when most were bundled up by their fire stoves in snowy cold Maine, Gary hit the waters and fished for lobster. This was our guy.

During the call to prepare Gary for his upcoming trip and appearance, we realized he was perfect. He spoke slowly and simply, he was humble and had a Maine accent like none other.

I told the 56-year-old Guy from Maine (as we now openly referred to Gary) to come to New York City as if it were "just another day at the office for him." In other words, I wanted him in full lobster fishing attire.

True to form, we brought cameras, self-reflecting on our own process as always, to the U.S. Airways terminal at LaGuardia Airport. When we couldn't find Guy from Maine (he hadn't been at an airport in forty years), I went to the U.S. Airways ticket counter to have him paged. The cameras rolled:

"Would the Guy from Maine with the smelly lobster suit please meet TV's Jake Sasseville by Passenger Pickup 1."

Moments later, Guy from Maine appeared. He towered over us at six-foot-five and his hands were so chapped from winters out on the Maine Sea that it hurt when we shook to say hello.

Guy from Maine joined me on an underground graffiti tour in Queens, a Japanese cross-dressing bar on the Lower East Side (revealed to him only after the man-on-man performance) and Guy from Maine replaced me in a segment where I instructed him on how to interview B-list Latin film star Octavio Gomez.

From left to right, Guy from Maine, Octavio Gomez and me, mid-segment on *The Edge.*

Our Ah-Hah moment

What we did best in those early days was create stuff out of what others saw as unimportant. No one asked questions like "What would happen if you put a 56-year-old lobsterman from Maine and a 24-year-old B-list film star from Nicaragua together in an interview, with a manic up-and-coming talk show host acting as coach?"

We layered segments and tried to introduce new ways of thinking about culture and society.

Of course, some people hated our show. They wrote in and they told us about it. But we didn't care. We loved it. Guy from Maine was one of the highest rated shows in our run. I remember my dad called me the next morning after the Guy from Maine episode aired and said how taking people from different backgrounds and bringing them together in awkward, albeit hilarious situations, was the show's true talent.

I think he was right.

Whores and Pimps

On one particularly challenging day of shooting, my talent producer Felicia booked Dennis Hoff, owner of the Bunny Ranch in Nevada. Actually, Felicia did a double-booking because Brooke, Dennis' "girlfriend," was also in town to promote their HBO show called "Cathouse."

I thought the premise was funny. Have a pimp and whore out with Jake on the streets of New York, announcing "open job interviews" for passers-by. After a series of double-entendre and open-ended questions like *How flexible are you? Do you like to make a lot of money? Would you like to retire in less than five years?* we'd reveal the *actual* job they were interviewing for by having Brooke, resident prostitute, stand up, take off her trench-coat and reveal a racy leather costume.

The problem was – I was a prude. I wasn't having much sex back then, and any sex talk made me uncomfortable. I was inexperienced and in the closet, fearful of what the world would think if I came out. And I found the idea of prostitution and promoting it deplorable.

I went along with the segment pitch and booking because my male producers *obviously* enjoyed the hit HBO show and I thought it'd be good for our ratings.

In the car, as we drove from their hotel to the set, the pimp Dennis Hoff was quiet, mostly busying himself on his blackberry. I sat in the middle of Dennis and Brooke, squished and uncomfortable, deathly afraid that Brooke was going to ask me about my sex life.

On the West Side Highway, Brooke whispered sweet nothings in my ear, offering to teach me a thing or two, insinuating that I knew nothing about sex. I was grossed out by her advances. She was a very pretty platinum blond with luscious lips and great big eyes, but I wasn't interested.

She grabbed at my groin. I yelped out of surprise. I dealt with uncomfortable situations by yelling at a producer.

"What the fuck, make her stop!" I instructed, sounding like I was in the fourth grade when Victoria Ramon cornered me and tried to kiss me.

Mark, my producer, looked at me as if to suggest that I was nuts. It wasn't the first time.

"Tell this broad to calm the fuck down!" I yelled again, after she grabbed me.

Mark did nothing, except laugh.

"Pull the goddamn car over!" I screamed as Brooke grabbed giggled.

No such request was honored. I had to cover my genitals and sit tight.

On set by NYU, as parent-child tours of the campus were passing by, I cringed as I grabbed my bull-horn and started the segment.

"Free interviews for a great job. Dental included!" I announced to onlookers. Sometimes my own personal discomfort made for the best comedy.

The reveal was funny but the gimmick of the whore taking off her trench coat and showing her lingerie got old real quick.

You will give that whore more airtime

We wrapped the segment and were just about to break for lunch when my executive producer Lori approached me.

"Jakey, listen honey," Lori said, in her motherly tone she used when she had to convince me of something. "We're going to need you to do a second segment with these guys."

I couldn't believe she would suggest such a thing after the morning's events. I told her how uncomfortable I was by the whole thing.

"We need to fill time because we're a little short, and your writers thought that since Brooke's life is based on taking photographs, that she could teach you a thing or two at a photo shoot."

Lori reminded me we needed a photo shoot for the new show anyways, and this could be two bird's down with one stone.

I had had a hard day and frankly was unimpressed that I was promoting legalized prostitution to an audience that I expected would be young. Also, I felt like a prude and wasn't seeing the comedy in all of this (even though in hindsight there was plenty).

"Absolutely not!" I said sternly, if only for effect. "I will not give this whore any more airtime!"

I flexed my executive producer muscle. I was the boss of this show.

Not this time.

"You *will* give that whore more airtime," Lori demanded, as her ushanka Russian hat slightly covered her eyebrows in twenty-degree weather.

"You can and will make this funny and interesting," Lori said as she pointed towards Brooke and Dennis, down the sidewalk. "Do we understand each other!?"

Suddenly, this wasn't so fun anymore. Creative brawls like this happen all the time making television. They just aren't usually about such ridiculousness.

"You cannot tell me what to do!" I yelled. "This is my goddamn show!"

"That's what you pay me for and you will be doing a second segment with these people," Lori snapped.

I wasn't going to win this one. As motherly as Lori was, she was *not* someone you wanted to cross. And I knew she wasn't pushing this onto me because she wanted to, but she had the bigger picture in mind. She was an excellent executive producer and had my back.

One of my camera guys hid behind a tree during our argument and captured the whole thing on tape. We put it in the episode.

I did the second segment at a photo studio and Brooke taught me how to pose like a whore for my photos. All in all, the final product was a pretty good segment. At the end of the photo shoot, Brooke confronted me as my staff packed up.

Cameras rolled.

"You really shouldn't judge people like me, Jake," she said, obviously sensing my prejudice.

"I just don't understand how you can do this to yourself," I shot back, relieving some tension with honesty.

"This is my body and I use it in the same way you use your TV cameras at work," Brooke said. "It's a business."

Thing is, she meant it. She saw her body as a tool in the same way my TV cameras were to me.

Pre-judgment is a virus

We also put this confrontation into the segment. It made it a complex and compelling five-minutes of television. Most revealing was how Brooke taught me how to approach a segment with as little judgment about whatever the situation is as possible. This has been a lesson that I've carried with me since.

People don't want to be judged. People want to be loved and respected. Their behavior may not be up to my standards, but that doesn't mean I can't find love and respect for them. Brooke taught me that I could speak with her fairly and equitably without endorsing or promoting what she did. It's the golden rule on steroids, and it was being played out on national television.

This is an old publicity shot for *The Edge* from 2008 from that photoshoot, sporting me and Brooke in a compromised position. One of us anyways.

We were willing to go those uncomfortable places. It's what made the show great. I learned a lot about creating a story in those early days. I learned about how to take care of my guests and how to keep judgment as far outside the equation as possible.

I wasn't playing games anymore, I was serious about my craft and about creating something spectacular. There was a game I was still playing though, and it was with the TV networks. It's a game I like to call...

14

A (DISNEY) CAT AND MOUSE GAME

Disney gets pissed, their lawyers harass me, my team celebrates, and how a smart marketing campaign can (and should) polarize people

In one respect at least the Martians are a happy people; they have no lawyers.

— EDGAR RICE BURROUGHS

After months of delay, *The Edge with Jake Sasseville* was set to launch on February 14, 2008.

I had just returned from filming the finale episode of *The Edge* in Las Vegas. The trip was part courtesy of my new and happy relationship with Air Tran Airways.

Despite arguing with Lori Fitch for three weeks over the trip, I did it anyway.

"Lori ," I pleaded. "What's the biggest cost of going to Vegas?"

"The plane tickets," she responded.

"Fine, Lori ," I shouted, making it sound as if this was a crucial decision, banging my hands on my desk. "I'll go get the goddamn tickets donated."

Lori smirked, knowing that I would. Our relationship was based on a tug-of-war. Lori told me why I couldn't do something, and then I'd figure out a way to do it.

Lori drank the "Jake Kool-Aid," but she also kept her distance so that she wouldn't be swept up in the grand illusion. My admittedly delusional thinking served my company and me well in the early days. It allowed us to attempt and achieve challenges many would consider impossible. It just wasn't grounded in enough experience to recognize the wisdom of being practical.

The problem was that eventually I'd fail. It was inevitable. And I had set up my whole high wire act without a safety net.

Delusions of grandeur

Within a week of the conversation with Lori, Air Tran Airways launched a significant partnership with us. As part of the inaugural campaign, they offered twenty round-trip first class airline tickets for my staff to Las Vegas.

I instructed the PR team to spin the success of the "Jake after Jimmy" campaign. We had tens of thousands of people who e-petitioned "I want my Jake after Jimmy on ABC" by January, 2008. Better yet, we were set to debut in 40 ABC markets in February.

Poor calculations

By February, I was done filming and I was mostly doing press. I was also trying to raise enough money to pay the $250,000 it'd cost to air my show after *Jimmy Kimmel Live*.

At the time I had only saved enough money for four episodes, trusting I'd come up with a plan by deadline. With four episodes worth of money in the bank, I also was faced with the prospect of not paying my staff. Again.

I trusted that the momentum of the show's launch would carry me through and help me close deals with advertisers.

How wrong I was.

Despite the financial challenges, my staff continued to work diligently. They trusted me to figure it out because I had countless other times before. Also, it helped that a New York Magazine article had just been released touting the launch of the show. The momentum helped craft perception that everything was going to be okay.

The article, written by Clancy Nolan, had been months in the making. Clancy was friends with my former head writer, Katie Bashinelli, who quit *The Edge* in November. Still, Clancy wanted to do the story and followed me and my staff around for months. Sometimes I'd walk into my office early in the morning, and somehow, Clancy would be sitting there, waiting, with no one there to let her in.

The article she ended up going to print with was scathing, but I tried to consider how no press was bad press.

The headline set it up: "Jake Sasseville is going to get an ABC contract even if it kills him."

The article read, in part:

> As executive producer, Jake, a 22-year-old with a Morrissey-style pompadour, is responsible for the bills. He's neither cool (he likes to do this goofy shoulder shimmy he calls the "Jake Shake") nor rich (he's the son of a teacher and a life coach), and he is raising the money for *The Edge* as he goes along. Now, eight weeks into filming and three months before the premiere, he's already out of cash. But Jake likes to characterize problems as "opportunities."
>
> ...In the meantime, part of the show's appeal is built around whether it'll make it at all. Tune into *The Edge* and watch a hyperactive kid careen toward fame or oblivion. See him plan his show in Queens (where, incidentally, he sleeps on a nearby deflated air mattress). Then gawk as mock triumph is followed by mock defeat. The camera rolls when Ford delivers a new car (Ford has signed a six-figure deal with *The Edge*), and is still rolling 24 hours later, after it's been towed.

....In January, Jake scores a short interview with Wyclef Jean at the Nokia Theatre in Times Square. I ask Jake if he's a fan. "Not until we booked him." Two index cards filled with Wyclef facts are tucked in his pockets, but he has no questions. "I think I'm just going to let it flow," Jake says, as he grabs a diet Red Bull. *The Edge* gets eight minutes of Wyclef's time, and Jake spends it mainly on small talk. He asks what it was like to work with Shakira and awkwardly tries out some slang he learned from Cipha Sounds. Wyclef obliges Jake with a quick, a cappella version of "If I Was President," and the interview ends. As the two men stand for pictures, Wyclef leans in and asks Jake if he's read much about Alexander the Great. "He conquered the world at your age."

New York Magazine, February 14, 2008

This is Wyclef Jean and I after the interview backstage at Nokia Theater in Times Square. Hands down, one of the best shows I've seen in a long time.

Later that day, I was in my office getting ready to do an ABC Newsinterview when my assistant Sasha came running into my office. She said it was urgent.

"Jake," she said. "I have Disney calling for you. They want to speak."

Even though I had prepared myself for this call for many years, I never thought it would happen this casually. I thought they were going to offer me a network deal.

"Jake's here," I announced, poised.

"Jake Sasseville?" the caller asked.

"Yes, how can I help?" I responded.

The caller identified himself as being with Disney's legal department. *Whoopsies.*

I listened carefully. I got excited, but became nervous.

"We're familiar with your 'Jake after Jimmy campaign', sir," the lawyer said sternly. "We cannot have you using Jimmy Kimmel's likeness or image in the way that you are doing."

I smirked.

Success meets resistance. Resistance causes friction. Intense friction creates pearls.

I had a democracy of young college kids pounding at the impenetrable doors of network late-night television, looking for every conceivable way in. Finally the scared executives inside opened the door just a crack, to see who was making all the noise.

When they found out it was a fresh-face college dropout, I imagine they were less than amused.

"Tell me more," I said, putting the burden on him to speak.

"We've seen that you have orchestrated an email campaign that is spamming our employees and Jimmy Kimmel's team, and while we acknowledge your creative approach, we are serving you with a 'cease and desist' letter and expect that you stop this behavior immediately."

Cease and desist - I'm not sure what to say.

I want to be respectful, but the rebel inside of me wanted to celebrate.

"Sure, no problem, have something drafted up and send it my way," I responded. "I'll make sure to have my legal team look at it."

"Sir, you don't understand," he interrupted. "We're asking you to stop your campaign immediately. Failure to do so will result in us having to take further action."

I pretended like he didn't just say that and went on with business as normal.

"Great, thanks so much, just send along the letter and I'll have a peek."
I'm the underdog. Take further action, fucker. Try it. I'd love the press.

I could imagine the headline: "Disney Sues 22-year-old TV guy who does a show after *Kimmel*."

I got lost in my thoughts. Unfortunately, I started to think any success I was experiencing was because of me. It's important to show up each day to do what it is you do, but equally important is to acknowledge that your success is not yours to own.

Turning a bad situation good, I ran to Brian's office, who was the 19-year-old in charge of our relationships with the ABC stations around the country.

"Brian! We did it! We did it! Disney is PISSED," I shouted.

I called my manager, Mark Schulman at 3Arts Entertainment in Los Angeles. I told him the story. Mark's brother was a senior executive at ABC in New York. I asked if he would make sure I wasn't in any legal trouble.

Ten minutes later, Mark called me back.

"Jakester," he said. "My brother would like you to come and meet him at his office. He and his associates want to have a chat."

"Good or bad?" I asked.

"All good, just go, he's a good guy," Mark said.

"Marky, I have an ABC interview today, I don't have time," I protested, half fearing that Mark's brother was going to actually kick my ass. I walked myself into it.

"It's in the same building," Mark said, laughing. "Just drop by his office after your interview."

Humorously, as Disney's lawyers were threatening to shut me down, I found out that Irv Schulman and his executive team at ABC were actually quite enthusiastic about my campaign and my show. His boss, Janice Marinelli, the president of Disney-ABC Domestic Television, apparently heard about me and was curious.

We got very lucky and we had great momentum moving toward our national debut, just as long as ABC didn't yank me off the air first.

It wouldn't be the last I'd hear about using Jimmy Kimmel's likeness and image. Except, next time, it'd come from Jimmy's people directly.

I had no time to focus on Disney lawyers, because I was too ecstatic that, finally, after months, blood, sweat and tears...

15

THE EDGE LAUNCHES ON VALENTINE'S DAY

Why valentine's Day 2008 was the gayest (and loneliest) day of my life.

Our manifestations and desires are meant to be ours, immediately, always. What takes so long for some of what we want to come into our lives is the amount of resistance we hold. Drop the resistance, and watch the near instant manifestations come.

–Jake Sasseville

During my ride in my new Ford Focus into Manhattan from Queens, I called Mark Schulman in Hollywood.

"Mark, I need a game changer," I said. "Can you set me up for a week of meetings with TV networks sometime in March while I'm out in LA?"

"I'll check when everyone is available," Mark responded.

On set of *The Edge,* me and my former head writer, James Murray, are hanging out in the Ford Focus that Ford gave us as part of the deal. I was so excited when I first drove the Focus to my office in SoHo, that I stuck my head outside the sunroof to greet my staff on the street, and unintentionally side swiped a parked van.

I'm always fascinated and humbled by people in my life so willing to help. Sure, Mark had skin in the game and an incentive to help me win. However, with clientele like Chelsea Handler, Mario Lopez, Rainn Wilson and Tyra Banks, I was low on the totem pole.

It's tough to win alone. It is imperative to enlist others for their help while finding ways to contribute to their life at the same time. It should always be a two-way exchange. Empower them to help you. People want to be a part of your success. Just ask.

The Edge with Jake Sasseville was set to launch on the day made for lovers, February 14.

Launch day was bookended with interviews. I met Ford execs for lunch as they checked up on their investment. No one knew that I was running out of money (again) and needed to find a way to pay the ABC affiliates $200,000 in less than three weeks.

How lonely.

Fox News nonsense

At 4:00 p.m. I hopped in the car Fox News sent for my publicists and me to go to the studio. The live show was at 5 p.m. The producer met me out front of Fox News studios and brought me for hair and makeup.

Rebecca Gomez, the show's anchor, was visibly afraid of me during the interview. In her defense, I was behaving out of control. I growled nervously, trying to break the ice and made questionable gestures toward her in the middle of the live interview.

I was trying to be friendly and entertaining, but instead came off as tactless and inappropriate. And I had no one to tell me otherwise. The show was live and there was no abandoning ship. For all intents and purposes, the actual interview was good and it told my story.

Gomez ended the interview asking me about my plans for the Valentine's Day.

"No plans, Rebecca," I said. "Are you saying you'd like to go out for a date?"

"Are you gay, Jake?" Rebecca asked, without hesitation.

Holy Fuck! Jesus Christ!

"No," I said nervously, losing eye contact for a moment as I lied.

That's what gay guys say when they're in the closet and terrified of coming out. They program their brain that if the word "gay" comes up in a question, you say "No." Immediately.

When I first met my friend Roseanne Barr in Los Angeles, she asked me if I was gay. I said no and she looked at me, curiously, knowing full well that I was gay but just hadn't come out. She was respectful and patient. After all, she had two siblings who were gay. Her fans are gay. Roseanne Barr knows gay.

Roseanne Barr and me sharing Brie cheese for lunch on a hot summer's day.

(I came out to Roseanne years later and she was pissed. Funny reaction. She remembered that I told her I wasn't gay years prior and told me I should've come out to her at the very least.)

To be honest, I was terrified about being gay.

I didn't think there could be a gay late night talk show host. I didn't know how I'd tell my family. I couldn't imagine having a boyfriend. I was terrified about everything that being gay meant. Yet I can't remember a time in my life when I didn't know I was gay. I knew.

I became a master at cloaking my sexuality. When an inquiry arose, I would subconsciously use that as an opportunity to bury my feelings and attractions towards men deeper and deeper. I thought that by burying them that I wouldn't be able to feel them.

I was hiding who I really was.

By doing so, I pushed all of the hurt and discomfort deep inside to the point where I couldn't feel real love. I felt hollow. Can you imagine not being able to recognize or feel real love? I felt like I couldn't become close with anyone, and that no one would let me in. My work was (and still is) my life. And I'm still learning even today how to allow myself to be loved.

My repressed emotions soon started to manifest themselves as aggression. And by "soon," I mean exactly ten-seconds after the Fox News interview, and gay line of questioning, ended.

I fired my publicist on the spot.

Why?

She should've known to stop the interview when they asked the gay question. Fuck, she should've told them at the beginning I don't want to talk about my sexuality.

But how was my publicist supposed to know? I wasn't out to anybody. I expected people to mind read.

This was the beginning of my unintentional megalomania. It was misplaced aggression triggered by a growing fear of who I really was.

I took the limo back to my office on Broadway solo and told the driver I'd be back in a few minutes. It turned into three hours.

I'm going to make Fox News pay for this car because of their fucking gay comment.

It was irrational but so was everything in my life. It was my way of showing the world who was boss. I felt helpless. It was supposed to be the biggest and best day of my life, but being asked if I was gay on national TV, with my family watching, dampened the celebration.

It was 11:00p.m. In Florida and Maine, *The Edge* was debuting. The rest of the country would see the show the next night. I was in my office, going through old notes, trying to figure out who I could call for help with my financial issues. I had no one to turn to.

I had no prospects for money and I owed people so much of it. I didn't know how I'd pay my staff or the ABC affiliates in the next few weeks. A sudden burst of sadness overcome me, as I lay on my beanbag and sobbed.

On the night when I should've been the happiest because all of my dreams were coming true, I was emotionally exhausted.

Family ties

As I tried to leave the office, my phone rang. It was my grandmother.

"Jake," the familiar voice said. "This is your grandma. I saw your show tonight. I am so proud of you my Jacob."

"Thanks, Grandma." I smiled, wiping away the tears. "I really love you."

She was my number one fan since I was a kid. I'd walk up and down her street, working her elderly neighbors like a comedy club, just to make her laugh.

Grandmom went on for ten minutes talking about each segment, detailing what she liked. Her and my aunt sent a giant plant that day to my office to congratulate me.

She was so happy that I was living my dream.

She had no clue how close I was to losing it all.

To hide my financial woes, I hid my checkbooks and avoided my executive producers. They stayed at the post-production facility in Long Island City, Queens, and I stayed in Manhattan. To hide my sexuality, I deepened my voice and acted straight in interviews. For me, they were inextricably linked. I wanted to hide from who I was becoming.

Winning in television

The week after *The Edge* hit the airwaves, the ratings were in and we were winning.

"We got a 10-share in Orlando!" Sasha, my faithful assistant, enthusiastically announced to all of us.

That means ten percent of the people watching television at the time my show aired in Orlando were watching *The Edge*. The ABC affiliate told us how improbable that was. Yet, we did it. And we did it again. Week after week.

"We've doubled our audience every week in New York!" Sasha screamed.

"And Oklahoma City says you've been pulling a 1.0 rating every single week."

I smiled. We put our work out into the world. We shipped it, months behind schedule, with bumps along the road and unsure of the future. Still, there was a fear that I'd lose it all, which brings me to the Fat Lady…

16

THIS FAT LADY AIN'T SANG YET

Fear of failure prompts risky business, cheeky chess moves and delicate maneuvers; none of which would work, but all of which were hella fun

In the city a funeral is just an interruption of traffic; in the country it is a form of popular entertainment.

— GEORGE ADE

I called Stormy Simon at Overstock.com.

"Stormy," I greeted her. "Jake's here."

"Jake," she responded. "Your ratings are up all over the country, and they are huge in Salt Lake."

"Yeah, cool huh?" I responded.

"And I'm thrilled that you're moving business at Overstock.com/Jake," Stormy said.

"Stormy, you advertise on that national NBC show called *In the Loop*, right."

"Sure," she said.

In the Loop was a national talk show that aired on NBC at noon weekdays from 2006-2008 live from Chicago.

"And you get to control the content that is created for the Overstock segment once a week right?"

I already knew the answer to my own question.

"Yuh, we work with the producers to create what goes on the show."

"I have an idea. I'd like to do a Generation Y spring break segment on *In the Loop* on NBC," I proposed.

It didn't take much convincing.

"Sure," she said. "That's a great idea."

"Great," I said. "And I'd like to do it in two weeks."

Stormy said she'd call the producers. I also asked her to meet me in Chicago, where the show was filmed live, to do appear with me. I knew she had a soft spot for being on TV, and a soft spot for me. She said yes.

"Thanks Stormy Simon! Love you!" I said.

I really did love her, like an older sister. She believed in me and we had a close relationship. She was one of the only executives that consistently and unapologetically saw me through the toughest growing pains in my business.

Hold your cards close to your chest

My plan, of course, was not to appear on the NBC show at all. Sure, I'd make the appearance. But, the real reason why I called Stormy Simon and asked her to book me on the show was because I needed to see her face-to-face to ask her to save my TV show.

I called Mark Schulman, my manager at 3Arts Entertainment, back in Hollywood.

"Mark, can you please confirm that these networks will meet us in two weeks? I'm heading to LA."

"I think that should work," Mark responded.

I told him I didn't care who we met with and that I just wanted to go to the top.

Even with the momentum three weeks into the thirteen-week run of *The Edge*, people were starting to lose faith. No new sales had hit the books. There was fanfare, but the smoke and mirror show was being revealed.

In post-production, we just edited the fourth episode and started working on the fifth. We had no money and thankfully my landlord allowed me to have a one month reprieve on my lease before kicking me to the curb.

"Sasha, please buy me tickets to Chicago and LA," I said. "And make a layover in Denver so I can go and meet with Crocs."

Maybe I could get Crocs to fund me.

We had done such a great job with them on the Crocs Next Step Campus Tour in the fall with the "Jake after Jimmy" campaign.

I called Max Duncan, who was the marketing head at Crocs.

"Max, it's Jake."

"What's up amigo?" he said.

Before I could say anything, he continued.

"Let me guess, you need money and you want me to help?"

Max knew me too well.

My relationship capital was starting to fray across the board. Unfortunately, I could only see a few steps ahead and couldn't understand the big picture to notice that I was starting to overextend my relationships and requests for help.

"I'm going to Denver, Max. Can you put your marketing team together for a presentation?" I asked.

"What about?" Max asked.

"About me, my show and the opportunity for investment," I responded. "I'll make it super clean and simple."

Though I hosted his Fall music tour, I never met the marketing executives at Crocs.

Max said that he didn't believe it would go anywhere, but if I wanted to fly out to Denver and make the presentation, he had my back.

I called Mark Schulman, putting heat on him to lock as many TV network meetings as possible.

"Mark, sorry to bother you again. I have an idea," I began.

Of course, I always have an idea.

"You manage Chelsea Handler, right?"

He said yes.

"And you executive produce Chelsea Lately on E!, correct?"

"I'm not booking you as a guest on Chelsea," Mark shot back, before I could even make the request.

I adjusted my strategy mid-sentence.

"Calm down, crazy man," I said. "Just book me on the panel at the beginning of the show with the comedians."

I wasn't a comedian. But I was crazy enough to think I could become one.

I wanted as big of an audience as possible to create a ton of buzz in the shortest amount of time, quickly.

Surely, something would pop.

"Hold on," Mark said.

Two minutes later he came back on the line. He had just called Chelsea's producers.

"This is a one-time thing, Jakester," Mark said. "You're booked."

I thanked him profusely.

"Jake," he said as he was about to hang up. "Whatever you do, be yourself, and don't try to out-Chelsea Chelsea. It doesn't work."

Within one afternoon, I had plotted my strategy.

I'd head to Chicago, ask Stormy Simon for $200,000 that I'd put toward Season 2 of *The Edge*, but actually use it for Season 1. I'd be honest about it with her, and would figure out a way to fund season 2 later.

If that didn't work, or even if it did, I'd ask Crocs for the same amount of money and then put it toward Season 2 for real. (This was, in all its tortured glory, a Ponzi scheme.)

Then, I'd go to Los Angeles, take meetings with all the major network executives, talk about our incredible show and success, and have to figure out which network offer I'd go with.

Whatever you think about how I did business in our early days, we certainly led from our hearts, but had our egos in it as well. We had to win. I had to win. I couldn't afford to fail. Not now.

Charity always looks good

I called Marcie Maxwell, who heads Communications at St. Jude's Children's Hospital in Memphis. I have a special fondness for St. Jude's and they were always very kind to me.

On a whim, I asked Marcie if any charity events were happening that week in Los Angeles for St. Jude's.

"Funny you should call, Jakey," Marcie said in her southern accent.

"We have a celebrity Scrabble Tournament fundraiser happening in the Hollywood Hills that Thursday night," Marcie said. "Red carpet and everything if you want to join."

Shit, I have to appear on Chelsea Handler on Thursday.

"What time, love?" I asked Marcie.

"Starts at 8 p.m.," Marcie told me. "And guess what? Jimmy Kimmel is hosting!"

Um. Excuse me?

"Marcie, are you serious?"

"Yeah, isn't that funny, since your show is after his and all," she said. "He's obsessed with Scrabble!"

"Can you book me to attend the event, pleeeaaasseee."

"Well, let me check if I can add you to the list," Marcie said, jokingly. "Look there, one last slot."

"Thank you Marcie!"

Shine a spotlight on your problems but only to distract on-lookers

Knowing how to get attention is an attractive skill that an entrepreneur must develop. This is especially true if you're facing defeat. Stack the chips, let it roll. It wasn't strategic but rather an impulsive way to play the game. I felt like I had no other choice.

I chunked it up to be a matter of fact. The more people talk about you, the more chance you have to get noticed, and the more chance you have to get business.

Appearing provocative also helped my case. It created a mysteriousness and intrigue around me and my brand and something that drew people closer. People asked a ton of questions. Journalists wrote about me.

Make sure your opponents don't always know what your next move is. Surprise them. It's thrilling and entertaining, and will be good for business.

I earnestly thought I could save my company. And I probably could have. Unfortunately, I wasn't aware of all the toes I stepped on in the last few months. Equally as mis-aligned, I started to fear losing it all, and brought that energy into my work. The joy and optimism that helped me create all the momentum gave way to dread and concern.

Perception is everything. The "paper trail" of appearances, meetings, celebrity interactions and press that I'd leave behind after my week in Hollywood would be strong enough so that when in front of the TV execs, we'd have a kick ass story to tell. Right? Before I'd get to Hollywood, though, I'd have to deal with...

17

A SHIT STORM(Y) IN CHICAGO

Wait a minute, Chief Marketing Officer Stormy Simon isn't in love with me? What the...

∽

The great corrupter of public man is the ego....Looking at the mirror distracts one's attention from the problem.

— DEAN ACHESON

It was the morning of my appearance on NBC's daytime gab fest *In the Loop*. Though I arrived in Chicago late the previous night, I was up early and ready to go.

Overstock.com rented an apartment in Chicago for guests of *In The Loop* and Stormy and I shared the apartment. She arrived after midnight.

We took a car to the studio together, catching up on the ride over. I was extremely nervous about the big ask I was about to drop on her.

Could she really consider a two hundred thousand dollar advance for the second season I thought nervously as we talked about Sundance.

I wasn't sure when the right time was to do it. Overstock.com was very happy with the sales that *The Edge* was generating for them, and especially that we were delivering a younger college-aged buyer, just like I promised to Stormy and Patrick, the CEO, months before.

Overstock also loved that I positioned them as the "hero" in my *David-and-Goliath-Jake-takes-on-the-TV-networks* story in all the media and interviews I did for the show.

A producer greeted when we arrived. He laid down the format of the show—segments, guests and cues—before walking us up to the second floor of NBC Tower in Chicago to hair and makeup prep.

It was fifteen minutes before the live show. Stormy was due to appear in the last part of the segment where the co-hosts and I would play Guitar Hero, sold at bargain rates on Overstock.com.

Corporate whore indeed.

I could hear the audience warm-up guy in the studio exciting the crowd of over 150 audience members. I didn't prepare for the segment on the show. I didn't care. I only had one thing on my mind. I had to figure out how to ask Stormy for $200,000.

Live television makes everything better

The activity behind the scenes is electric. Cell phones rang, producers screamed and other distractions added to the brilliance of this controlled chaos. My heart raced – not for the live show in front of millions of people, but for another reason.

I have to ask Stormy for this goddamn money. Just do it.

I had such anxiety in those few moments backstage, waiting to go on, knowing full well I needed to ask her immediately since she was leaving on a plane directly after the show.

Stormy and I were facing floor to ceiling windows overlooking Chicago when I leaned into the discomfort, prepared to jump in.

"Did you get my email," I asked Stormy, breaking my silence.

"No, what email?" she asked.

Fuck. She didn't receive the email.

"The email I sent about requesting the advance on the second season."

"Jake, what the hell are you talking about?"

"Stormy, I need $200,000 by next week in order to keep my show on the air."

"You didn't tell me this," Stormy quipped.

"I just did. And I emailed you two days ago."

I was only making things worst. She must not have received the email?

"I know it's a lot, but...."

"Jake," she said, cutting into my melodramatic soliloquy. "Only four episodes of your show have aired and we bought thirteen in total. How am I going to give you an advance?"

"I don't know," I said, trying to ease the tension. "I'm really stuck and you guys have always been there for me."

This was another big business lesson for me. A series of unreciprocated favors is detrimental to a partnership. Overstock.com and Stormy went to bat for me and gave my show wings. But they didn't have to. The relationship I worked hard to build started to crumble that day in Chicago. I was speeding the implosion by acting entitled.

"Jake and Stormy you're needed on set now," a producer screamed from down the hall.

We walked briskly toward the studio. We heard the audience cheer as the show came back from commercial break.

"Do you think you can do it?" I whispered.

"I need to check with the accountants tomorrow," Stormy replied, looking past me.

The sound guy reached up our shirts to mic us.

"How likely is it?" I asked Stormy, frustrated.

"Move your ass!" the producer screamed.

I was being groped and yelled at, and still trying to get Stormy to commit to the $200,000. I wouldn't let it go.

The producer grabbed my arm.

"Go, go," she pointed toward the stage.

I looked back at Stormy for an answer.

"I don't know Jake, I'll see what I can do," Stormy said.

"Four, Three, Two...." the slightly overweight stage manager yelled.

And just like that, I was on TV, fully unprepared. I talked with Ereka Vetrini and Bill Rancik, co-host of *In the Loop* and former contestants on *The Apprentice*, about Overstock.com products for generation Y and spring break. A dog and pony show at best.

The segment ended.

The good news was that Stormy's Blackberry lit up with favorable results from the appearance. Sales were up on products I talked about.

Maybe I have a career as a pitchman if this thing collapses.

I explained how sorry I was for sideswiping her before the show.

"I'm going to go back to Salt Lake City today and I'll call you about this tomorrow," Stormy said as she got into the car. "It was really great seeing you Jake!"

"Unbelievable as always, Storm," I said.

Cancelled

As I stepped onto my plane to Denver, Sasha emailed me a link online that announced that *In the Loop* had just been cancelled. The show would wrap production in a few months. The ratings weren't strong enough. Stormy was the first advertiser to commit to that show, too.

I flew to Denver and met with Max Duncan from Crocs. It was business as usual, but all I thought about was Overstock.com. I prayed that Stormy would say "YES" one more time. I couldn't focus on my presentation to the Crocs marketing team because I was distracted.

Max called me after the meeting.

"Jake," he said. "They really like you, but they're cutting their spending across the board."

He told me Crocs stock had just fallen from $70 a share to $7 a share. They wouldn't be able to do business with me.

I never experienced a failure like this before. It was a pro-longed fall from grace and still unclear from where I stood that day in Denver if it was failure or just a minor hiccup. I took credit for my surge of success, if not publicly then certainly privately, when really my success and failure has nothing to do with me. And yours has nothing to do with you. I learned to acknowledge that I'm simply a channel for which my creations flow through.

My job, then, is not to focus on succeeding or failing, but making sure, through meditation, healthy eating, getting curious about everything, treating people well, seeking out mentors, yoga and all else, that I am open and honest and clear and detached from the outcome.

I had a funny feeling that I was about to learn some very difficult lessons. I had a funny voice in my head saying, however quiet, that this was...

18

THE BEGINNING OF THE END

The anxiety of what failure brings is actually worse than the doom itself.

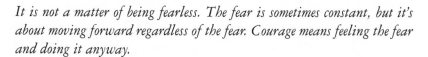

It is not a matter of being fearless. The fear is sometimes constant, but it's about moving forward regardless of the fear. Courage means feeling the fear and doing it anyway.

— GILLIAN ANDERSON

That night in Denver, after Crocs passed I got a call from my executive producer in New York City.

"I don't know how long I can keep people working for you," Lori said. "The staff is getting really agitated."

At that point, I owed most of them at least six weeks' pay—a sum of $120,000.

"Everything is going to be fine," I promised. I sensed I started to disbelieve it myself.

"I'll be in LA tomorrow with Mark Schulman to meet with the networks. Something's going to happen."

Lori was silent.

"Just *please* keep everything moving."

I hung up after we said goodbye.

Fear of failure paralyzes most.

The moment you lose your focus mentally, it becomes very difficult to recover. I tossed and turned as I tried to fall asleep in Denver that night. I thought about Stormy and hoped I'd wake up to a miracle in the morning.

Domino Effect

The next morning, I got a call from Stormy Simon.

A few minutes of small talk was my attempt to avoid any looming rejection. Stormy got to the point.

"Listen, Jake. I am really, really sorry. I cannot do this for you."

I lost hope. Thoughts raced as Stormy's words started to blur. I put the cart before the horse and thought I had the Midas touch. I started to buy into my own hype. And now it's crumbling.

Russian Roulette with ABC

Besides Stormy and Crocs saying NO, I placed a bet the night before that one would say YES. I instructed my assistant Sasha in New York to write advance checks to ABC in order for *The Edge* to air that week (the fifth episode). If the ABC stations didn't receive the checks, they wouldn't air the show. Instead of sending the checks I told Sasha to fax a copy to the ABC stations, suggesting that "payment was on its way."

That way, the stations would air that week's show without interruption.

I hedged with ABC affiliates, but now they were expecting to receive the check in two days, the sum of which is $25,000. And both of the people

I thought would help me with the cash were passing. Without any money committed, I couldn't send checks because they'd bounce.

All at once, I lunged myself into more than $25,000 of debt and I single-handedly wrecked relationships with 40 powerful ABC stations and their general managers nationwide.

The other problem with the ABC stations was that most required a two-week cancellation clause. Therefore, they'd air a repeat the *following week* as well, and charge me for it. So that $25,000 bet I made just doubled to $50,000.

It was not my finest moment. I did more damage to my reputation in the television industry in those 24 hours than most could do in a lifetime. And I was still only 22-years-old.

Fuck me.

"If you need to take some time off, we will support you," Stormy continued. "But we simply cannot do this right now."

My voice quivered as I thanked her and hung up the phone. I tried to find reasons to be grateful. It was hard. I was physically exhausted and emotionally torpedoed. My head hung low as I packed my bags and went to the airport.

I flew to Los Angeles that afternoon. I didn't mention a word of what happened that morning to my manager Mark Schulman. I knew it would kill momentum. Mark scheduled meetings with the top TV Network presidents and decision makers. I still had a chance. I hadn't tapped into one group of people that could change it all. That group of people is my...

19

HOLLYWOOD ENTOURAGE

Why I don't like being compared to Tom Green and an exclusive bird's eye view of what happens when a human being is torn apart, piece by piece, inside out.

~~~~~~~

We have long observed that every neurosis has the result, and therefore probably the purpose, of forcing the patient out of real life, of alienating him from actuality.

— SIGMUND FREUD

It was Monday morning in Los Angeles.

This week would be the last week that *The Edge* would be on the air for over 14 months. I drove to Mark's office in a car I borrowed from Ford, having not a clue in the world how I got in this mess, nor how to get myself out.

Scott, Mark's assistant, told me we had thirteen meetings with network executives that week. I saw it as an opportunity for an unordinary breakthrough in a series of devastating blows. I believed it was possible.

Mark ran down the laundry list of meetings as we cruised down Wilshire Boulevard in his Range Rover. The brass from ABC and NBC, the syndication president for Paramount Pictures, VH1 and MTV executives and a slew of other potential international distributors, financiers and executives were in our schedule.

I can still turn this around.

I obsessed about keeping hope alive. Did I have another choice?

VH1 forgets one. Jake Sasseville

Our very first meeting that week was with Stacy Alexander, senior vice president of talent and casting, at VH1. When we met, she acted like it was our first time meeting. It wasn't.

Stacy first met me in 2005 when she was a junior development executive during a memorable, if not eccentric, exchange between myself, her and her boss, Stella Stopler. Stella was the senior vice president of Celebrity Talent and Development. Robert Flutie, my manager at the time, set us up for a meeting.

Stella liked me. A lot. After ten minutes of discussing my (non) qualifications for being on VH1 at the ripe old age of 19, and my vision for the future of television, Stella saw something in me. I hit her soft spot or mildly entertained her, or something like that. In any case, at one point she was so moved that she leaped half of her body, led by her bosom, onto the conference room table to dial my manager Robert Flutie.

It was all very dramatic for a kid from Maine that just wanted a TV show.

"Robert, it's Stella, I'm here with Jake," Stella said assertively into the phone. It wasn't on speaker.

"This kid is un-fucking believable," Stella said, as Stacy Alexander, to Stella's direct right, smiled, nodded and agreed. "Where has he been all my life?"

My heart raced as I saw that I struck a nerve.

"We should do something with this kid in development on Best Week Ever or something," Stella said, then quickly changed the subject. "Yea, yea, okay, I'll call you later to set it up. I'll see you at the party"

She hung up the phone.

We talked for ten more minutes and I felt great. She said she'd call Robert Flutie to discuss specifics. The next night, I was at Robert Flutie's house in Pacific Palisades, California for a Holiday party.

Many of the executives I met the day before were there including Stella, Leigh Collier from Telepictures and Holly Jacobs from Paramount. Stella came up to me and told me how fabulous I was. She said she'd speak with Robert the following week to roll forward.

She never called. Ever. Welcome to Hollywood.

Now in 2008, with my new manager Mark Schulman by my side, and after some awkward probing, Stacy sort of remembered the dramatics of 2005. Unfortunately for Stacy, though, (and everyone else in the room) I talked circles around her and her development people. I was so wound up on adrenaline that, while they tried to keep up, it was clear that I wouldn't be the right fit for VH1.

We left the office.

"Jake, you need to calm the hell down with people like that," Mark said as we left Stacy's office. "They have no clue what the you're talking about."

I thought it was odd, since I was only speaking television jargon. Wasn't that their business?

Mark called his assistant and told him to change the MTV meeting we had scheduled for that afternoon.

"What the fuck are you doing?" I frantically interrupted him.

"I'm changing the agenda at MTV so we meet with different people, because you obviously need a real executive to handle you," he said.

Mark was in his car on the phone as I powered through a garden salad in between meetings.

The machine runs out of gas

My phone rang. It was my producer Lori Fitch .

"Jake, we are done," she said. "We simply can't continue."

First Crocs passes. Then Stormy says no-go. Then I double-down on my ABC bet and lose. Now my team quits on me.

"I can't keep these people working," Lori said. "They are concerned, they are scared, and they need to find other jobs, Jake. They can't pay rent."

Lori said that they would do everything to support me, but they couldn't keep the machine running. The gears were too damaged.

"We are going to put all the tapes and equipment in boxes," she assured me. "We are going to move stuff out of the office. People have to find work elsewhere."

My heart broke in half.

I let everyone down. I wanted to fix the situation and couldn't figure out how. That was probably the most frustrating. I was willing to do anything it took to fix the problem. I just didn't know what I didn't know.

I never thought I'd lose the staff. The only option was for more money to come in, right? The staff quit. I often saw them as an insurance policy, keeping things on track so I could focus on generating more income. It turns out all insurance policies have a premium.

There is great wisdom in detaching. That is, detaching from the outcome you intend to create. By detaching, you allow more possibility to flow in. You give yourself permission to create more. You allow yourself to feel the journey.

I was manic about trying to save the show and expected everyone around me to be as manic. That's just not the way the world works, I learned.

I quickly did the numbers and recognized that with my staffing costs, the ABC costs and other vendors, I owed $250,000.

My mind raced.

I was on the air for only five weeks.

What would I tell Ford?

I thought about Kurt in Detroit who told me that he couldn't afford "for this not to work."

Mark and I rode to Burbank to meet with NBC to discuss our success and our vision for late night. This was going to be torturous, if not deluded. Fatigue set in.

Maybe NBC can save me

Mark and I met with Rick Ludwin, a 28-year NBC exec who was in charge of late night programming. He was responsible for the promotion of Jay Leno in 1993 (instead of David Letterman) and presided, in part, over the Conan/Jay Leno fiasco in 2009. He also oversaw Saturday Night Live and other NBC special programming. Without Rick, there would have been no Seinfeld. Without Rick, Conan would never have been picked to replace to David Letterman in 1993. He's a legend in the entertainment business.

It was a lovely one-hour meeting, and for just a moment I found relief in speaking with Rick. He applauded my efforts and my success, and suggested that while I wasn't the right fit for NBC, that I consider really finding my on-camera voice instead of being scattered. He suggested focus in developing my "shtick" and shared that he thought I was "all over the place." This was welcomed advice. I was touched and grateful.

After the NBC meeting, we headed for our last meeting of that day, with Debmar-Mercury. My frustration reached boiling point as I saw the text messages from my team who were very concerned. Sasha texted and said the ABC stations wanted their money.

Caution: Boiling point is not flattering

Our next meeting was with a syndication company called Debmar-Mercury. Ira Bernstein and Mort Marcus, two former heads of the Walt Disney Company, founded Debmar.

They were responsible for syndication of *The Wendy Williams Show, The Tom Green Show, The Jeremy Kyle Show and The Man Show,* among others.

Curiously, the Debmar-Mercury executives were impressed by my recent surge of success and PR. It was when they drilled into my business model that they began to grow skeptical. They had every reason to be. It all seemed too good to be true. Because it was.

About thirty minutes into the meeting, Ira and Mort shared with me how much I reminded them of Tom Green. They produced *The Tom Green Show*. They compared me to Tom and then proceeded to tell me how much money they lost by investing in him. It was a failure and they were battle wounded.

I blew a fuse, furious that I was being compared to Tom Green.

"Fuck Tom Green," I shouted. "What's wrong with you people?"

Mark looked at me. He was shocked. I was shocked. I had never had outbursts like this.

Fuck this.

"Are you going to sit on your big asses in your Santa Monica offices and tell me I remind you of fucking Tom Green? Just look at me!"

The question was rhetorical, but I expected an answer.

The two execs sat in silence.

The tirade continued.

"I've just spent *years* of my life (exaggeration) creating a *revolution* in late night (double exaggeration added for effect). You guys are the whole fucking problem to the industry."

I didn't really mean that, but I also didn't pull back.

"I am one of the most brilliant minds in this business and I'd appreciate some fucking respect."

I felt good for a moment. Then I realized I just ruined everything. Again. With more important people.

These are not the Hollywood types you want to provoke in a fight. Word travels fast, especially when you have a loose cannon firing shots all around town.

It was too late. I didn't only burn the bridge, I blew it to smithereens. So instead of waiting for a response from Mort or Ira, I instead decided to deploy one of my classic pattern interrupts.

"And now, if you'll excuse me," I gathered myself, "I have to go pee."

This is what it looks like to be ripped to shreds from the inside out. It felt horrible to act out in this way, and I didn't feel like I had any control to stop it. I was embarrassed and furious.

I apologized for my temper tantrum when Mark came downstairs. I explained how *The Edge* couldn't afford to continue and was being taken off the air. I told him I felt like I had no one to turn to.

"Don't apologize to me," Mark said. "Go back upstairs and tell them."

I did.

I went upstairs and asked to meet Mort and Ira. I explained that I was under a lot of stress and thanked them both for meeting with me and how sorry I was for the outburst.

They said it was quite all right, and they wished me good luck.

And now, for a question and answer session from our sponsors...

20

Q: WHAT CUTS SHARP ON CONTACT AND LOOKS BETTER IN PERSON THAN ON TELEVISION? A: "AS SEEN ON TV" GINSU KNIVES

Why it took the 2E! Network three months to pay me after my appearance on Chelsea Lately

~~~⌒~~~

Tact is the ability to describe others as they see themselves.

— ABRAHAM LINCOLN

Later that day I was due to appear on *Chelsea Lately*. They filmed the show promptly at 5:00 p.m. I needed something to numb the pain of the day.

Instead of alcohol, I downed Red Bulls and Diet Snapple Iced Teas. I figured the iced teas balanced the intensity of Red Bull.

With the liquid jolt of guarana and caffeine coursing through my veins, I showed up to the studios at West Olympic in Los Angeles an hour early. The production offices were modern, white and carpeted. Chuy walked past me as I headed for the dressing room. I liked *Chelsea Lately* and couldn't believe I was going to be a panelist.

One million people a night tune in. The idea of trying to be funny by making fun of celebrities, the premise of the show, scared the shit out of me.

(Full disclosure: While I was the one who made the call to Mark Schulman to book me on Chelsea, it was one of my employees who pushed me to do it. I really didn't want to. I could feel the resistance. Even after I was booked, I was hesitant. You should always follow your intuition. The following is what happens when you do not listen to your inner voice.)

I settled down in the green room, trying to gain my composure. On my desk, a spread of tabloid press clippings lay before me. These were the topics du jour we were discussing.

The *Chelsea Lately* producers presented me with topics to review before the roundtable. Here's what "made news" in 2008.

Chelsea Lately
Roundtable Notes for Jake Sasseville

1) Lindsay Lohan and Samantha Ronson update. They've been re-'outed' – the first time by Lindsay's dad and now by Sam's brother – who told the media that make a 'cute couple.' It's also said they're looking for a place to buy. And, remember when Lindsay told Ashley to keep her 'Full House ass away from my girlfriend?' Well, it was actually Mary Kate she told off – who's now freaked out because she doesn't want people to think she's a lesbian!

2) Spencer and Heidi want to have a televised wedding...but NO ONE CARES! They want it to be held on Sir Richard Branson's island, with catering by Wolfgang Puck's 'Cut', U2 performing, and a watch giveaway by Jason of Beverly Hills – WHY DO THEY THINK THEY ARE CELEBRITIES?

3) George Clooney's ex Sarah Larson is said to have gotten a boob-job JUST before he dumped her. Ironically, he's been quoted saying he's NOT a boob-man.

4) Naomi Campbell wants to have a baby, and says she'd even do it without a father. She thinks it would calm her down...HUH? Why do all these celebrities (like Paris Hilton) think they can just have babies – as if it were like buying a new handbag? Also, she was just spotted by TMZ falling down after leaving a party...girlfriend is a mess!

5) Angelina told Entertainment Weekly that those mysterious tattoos on Brad's lower back don't mean anything – she just doodled on him one day, and he had her drawings tattooed on, permanently! Also, Maddox is very into drawing war scenes with lots of guns (creepy). Brad took one of his machine gun drawings and had it made into a gold necklace for Angelina (also creepy). She also says she's friends with her exes...like Billy Bob (remember that?).

6) According to CNN, a lot of people are tired AND SLEEP at work. Many offices have now even built nap rooms...is this a good idea? Jenifer Aniston and Martha Stewart are just two of the celebrities that claim they NEVER sleep...why do you think they don't?

7) Jackson's update. Tito – just kidding, there's not one. Michael – he's making a clothing line! What do you think it will be like / include? Janet – drops and gains weight more than Carnie Wilson, AND the European leg of her new tour was just cancelled!

8) Britney Spears and Mel Gibson were spotted hanging out again – this time at the exclusive cigar club, Havana. WHAT DO THEY HAVE TO TALK ABOUT? Also, it's said she wants to have a baby girl with K-Fed...does ANYONE think that's a good idea? Does K-Fed?

Ryan, the associate producer for *Chelsea Lately*, entered.
"Hi Jake, are you all set with what you're talking about?" Ryan asked.

No one told me that I would be working with prepared content.

"Sure," I lied, as I downed another Red Bull. Every cell in my body was jittering.

Ryan explained to me Chelsea relies heavily on her panelists to have funny stuff to say.

I was supposed to pull funny observations out of the topics and make it appear off the cuff.

I was in way over my head. This isn't what I do. I don't make fun of celebs. I'm not a comedian. And Chelsea Handler scares the shit out of me.

Still, I decided I wouldn't quit.

"What do you think about what happened to Lindsey?" Ryan quizzed.

Fuck you, Lindsey Lohan.

"Um, yeah, I don't want to really blow my load prematurely," I told him. "Rather be more spontaneous."

Ryan moved on, trying to humor me.

"And what about Michael Jackson launching a new line of pajamas for kids?" he asked, hooking me for my stance.

"Hah, yeah!" I said hesitantly, "What is he going to call it, MJ's PJs?"

I got a chuckle of approval. I rolled my eyes and almost cried.

I heard a noise coming from the other dressing room that sounded like laughter.

I recognized Arden Myrin from *MadTV* on Fox. She was another panelist.

Not only am I not a comedian, but I'm going to be on this show with *real* comedians. It's ironically funny when you consider that I could've just avoided this whole headache had I thought about this before asking Mark to book me on the show. It's as if I like to play with fire.

My heart raced. After Ryan left, not amused by my unpreparedness, I sat there, starring at myself in the mirror, watching my pupils dilate.

Arden Myrin and her associate producer, meanwhile, were cackling next door.

I wish that could be me.

I felt raw and empty inside. I saw that night's guest, Ashanti, with her entourage enter her dressing room.

That's me backstage at Chelsea Lately.

I decided I'd go and mingle with Arden and Ashanti. As I was stepping out of my dressing room, Chelsea Handler cut in front of me.

"Hi Jake," she introduced herself. "Thanks for coming in."

I shook her hand and thanked her for having me. I backed up back into my dressing room.

I sat down and she leaned up against the desk. Chelsea and I exchanged small talk about Los Angeles and sharing the same manager. She was very kind.

Then I said something that defied logic.

"Chelsea, you should do more in person appearances. You look a lot skinnier in person than you do on TV," I said, like a jackass.

Fucking Red Bulls.

"Oh, you think so," she said disdainfully, sharply cutting off the conversation. She adjusted herself in my mirror. "Aren't you funny?" She walked away.

Obviously, not.

Then I remembered what my manager Mark Schulman, who also managed Chelsea, told me prior to the appearance—*"Whatever you do, Jake, don't try to out-Chelsea, Chelsea."*

The next thirty minutes would be the most painful of my career. I'd get a grand total of two laughs from the audience (one was a sympathy laugh).

During the commercial break, the associate producers approached the stage to chat about the segment. Ryan, my producer, on the other hand, was so embarrassed that he stayed backstage.

I just couldn't keep up. MJs PJs was the only real laugh. The only one. I bombed in front of a million people and Chelsea didn't much care.

I left the studio and headed to the Hollywood Hills. It was the perfect setting for what was about to be...

21

THE FINAL BLOW

Why failure ain't so bad after all, especially when it's with Jimmy Kimmel by your side

Only a man who knows what it is like to be defeated can reach down to the bottom of his soul and come up with the extra ounce of power it takes to win when the match is even.

— MUHAMMAD ALI

Last on the list was St. Jude's Children's Hospital's Celebrity Scrabble fundraiser in the Hollywood Hills.

I received an email telling me that Jeff Probst, host of *Survivor*, Andy Richter from *Conan*, Andy Dick, Seth Green and Paul Rudd would be in attendance and that I needed to be on my "best behavior."

I arrived to see a modest group of photographers snapping away at the celebrities strolling down the red carpet. I followed suit. Why not? I'm a big star. In my head anyways.

I painfully walked down the red carpet and no one took my picture. I prayed someone would mistake me (like they usually do) for Perez Hilton or Jack Black.

Two dozen photographers and not one picture.

I am torturing myself.

I took my bruised ego and my sorry ass into the party. I invited my childhood friend Ezra to attend with me.

Play the game

Jimmy Kimmel was hosting the evening's festivities. Kimmel is a self-proclaimed Scrabble king. People paid big money to St. Jude's to get access to the event and to play Scrabble with celebs. Even though I was next to Kimmel, I couldn't say anything to him. After my day of mishaps and misguided aggression, I figured it probably was best just to observe.

As I watched Andy Richter kick Jeff Probst's ass at one Scrabble table, Kimmel was playing Seth Green to their right. I watched both games. Just then I noticed a woman standing next to me.

"Hello," I said as I shifted my body toward her. "How are ya?'

She smiled. She was homely, simply dressed and unusually calm. She provided a nice break from the Hollywood glamour.

"What are you doing? Who are *you* supporting?" I asked.

She pointed at Jimmy Kimmel.

"I'm with THAT guy," she said.

"That's odd, you don't look like Sarah Silverman," I said.

She chuckled.

"No, no, no, I'm his executive producer."

Oh no.

I started laughing. She looked at me oddly. I guess no one usually laughs at the comment "I'm his executive producer."

But I knew that chances were that this was the woman we had spammed tens of thousands of emails to with "I want my Jake after Jimmy on ABC" six months prior.

I realized when she told me her name was Jill that indeed this was *the* Jill Liederman on our email list.

"Is your last name Leiderman?" I asked, knowing the answer.

"Yes it is," she responded. "Who are you?"

"My name is Jake, it's nice to meet you," I said.

I looked for her to recognize me. She didn't.

"You used to work with Stew Bailey at *The Daily Show with Jon Stewart*, right?"

I couldn't resist interrogating further, even though I knew where this was headed.

"Yeah, I love Stew," she said. "How do you know him?"

"He worked with me on my talk show."

Hook, bait... and time to sinker (sink her).

"Oh you have a talk show?" Jill acted surprised.

Maybe it's not her?

"Yeah, it actually airs right after your guy in a bunch of ABC markets." I said, pointing to Kimmel, who was spelling the word "Disjointed" on the Scrabble board.

"You're Jake," she said, finally recognizing me. "You're Jake after fucking Jimmy," she said a little louder, surprised.

I smiled.

"Hi. Nice to meet you."

You just had to go there didn't you, Sasseville. You couldn't let sleeping dogs lie.

Then, in a complete surprise move, Jill confronted me not about the campaign or spamming her, but about using Jimmy Kimmel's 'likeness and image' without permission.

"You didn't have to use his likeness or image," said Jill Liederman, referring to Kimmel. "You could have just done this on your own."

This is so fucking surreal. I am being torn apart by the executive producer of Jimmy Kimmel—in front of Jimmy Kimmel—at a celebrity Scrabble tournament.

I was so tired that I didn't even care. I reveled in the attention.

Even though I should have been terrified to piss off Jill Liederman, I was actually relieved. Hearing that our grassroots marketing campaign "Jake after Jimmy" was effective put a smile on my face and thrilled me.

It was a confirmation that even in the light of being cancelled that week and facing a probable bankruptcy, I pierced the TV network system and somehow broke through.

All was not lost.

What being an entrepreneur really means

I had so much love and gratitude for my small team of unconventional thinkers back in New York City that night in the Hollywood Hills. They had the naiveté and gravitas to dream with me that there was something different that we could create together in television.

The lunatics were turning the asylum on its head and Nurse Ratched was livid.

I think this is the glory that many entrepreneurs seek. Yet, it manifested itself for me at an intimate party without fanfare or recognition. It was a whisper that came in after Jill's roar.

Whatever happened next didn't matter. The story of "Jake after Jimmy" and rallying my generation behind me and making the TV show more about the audience than about me, re-ignited a sense of idealism and what I was actually capable of. In the midst of failure, rejection and being cancelled, somehow there was light still shining in the tunnel.

Disrupting network television's "business as usual" model is just my personal example.

How can you be disruptive? Stop defending the status quo. What are you willing to do to stir a reaction like those we got from Jill Liederman and Disney?

Journalist and author Laurence Bass once said about me in an article readied for the New York Times:

"All revolutions are started by a faceless figure in the crowd."

If that is indeed true, then everyone reading this book can be a revolutionary. It starts with one person, one act of kindness, one fearless leader who is usually unknown, but is determined and focused enough to turn up the stakes and live passionately from within.

Embracing what you know makes you different

I knew that we were preempting change. I could feel it. I didn't know how or when, but I knew we had reached a peak (literally) atop the Hollywood Hills, overlooking Los Angeles on that bright starry night.

This wasn't about one or two isolated stories of success or failure, but the larger story of disrupting the system and re-writing the rules and how gratifying it is to create something uniquely you but also something that touches everyone else around you.

I've embraced the fact that my calling is to be a state-changer. Think about those in your life that mean the most to you. And think about, just for a moment, why they mean so much to you.

It's probably because they change your state. They bring you to a place of joy or happiness, reflection or awareness. Those people in your life that mean the most to you are the people who bring out the best in you.

For me, instead of disregarding the impact I have on people's lives, I'm choosing to embrace it, with all of my flaws and shortcomings included.

The best defense is a good offense.

I'm slowly mastering the art of influence, but not by coercing people to do things that they don't actually want to do. That never works long term. Instead, I help get people where they want to be. I argue it's not about the convertible or the big house that you want, but it's how you want to feel when you get there.

One of my deepest desires is to help people recognize that they can _**feel good now**_, regardless of their circumstances, and that feeling good will help to create everything they want.

I see the very best in people even if they don't see it in themselves. That's the only way my team was able to cause such chaos and interruption at ABC and Disney with the "Jake after Jimmy" campaign.

We were a group of fresh-faced 20-somethings who had no experience. We only had an eagerness to disrupt and change the status quo.

I had to empower my team to believe more in themselves than even they did because I couldn't afford a more experienced staff. I worked with what I had, and looking back, I wouldn't have changed any of it. We created a dent in the universe because we *thought* we could, and we acted from that place of certainty.

Controlled chaos in the cosmos

I completely lost my footing and fell down that day in 2008. I acted out and wasn't proud of my behavior. But that didn't change what we accomplished. The "Jake after Jimmy" e-petitions, the 1,250,000 people that watched the first season of *The Edge* and the thrill of impacting people's lives.

Those results still stood. And they'd help me start over.

What is *your* genius? We all have one. What is something that you can do that no one else can?

After my run-in with Kimmel's producer, I excused myself and retreated to a quiet place in the house. I called my staff in New York who worked on "Jake after Jimmy" and shared the story with them. They were delighted and thrilled by my run in. We had all made this happen together.

I re-joined the party an hour later and watched my childhood friend Ezra help Jeff Probst win an epic game of Scrabble. I let go of all my anxiety and partied the rest of the night away.

PART TWO
THE FREEDOM OF THE FALL

Why failing doesn't mean you're a failure, and the anecdotes, strategies and balls-out approach I used to stage a come back

22

BEING IN A STATE OF ACCEPTANCE

When you fail, no one seizes your house or your children (I had neither), but a landlord will deadbolt your office door shut (crap!)

It is wrong to think that misfortunes come from the east or from the west; they originate within one's own mind. Therefore, it is foolish to guard against misfortunes from the external world and leave the inner mind uncontrolled.

— BUDDHA

I returned to New York and prayed that someone from a network—any network—would call. Surely my effort in Hollywood the week before would pay off in some way, shape or form.

No one called. Not a one.

My landlord extended an extra month to me in my Soho office (or did that only happen in my head?) and I figured it was time to pack up. I wasn't quitting. I just knew I couldn't afford the rent.

I scrolled through my phone to text friends and see if they could help me move.

Only one person responded. Manuel.

When I called him, I could hear in his voice that he was hesitant to help me. He knew everything that (didn't) happen in Los Angeles, and that I was being forced out of my office. It wasn't a surprise to him. Still, his hesitance was sobering. There was something I couldn't pinpoint in his voice. Something that seemed to tell me there was another tough lesson I was about to learn. He agreed to help me after I explained the how much I needed him.

My head hung low as I walked down to my office on Broadway. It was a warm spring day in April. The loneliness of failure is all consuming. No friends and no staff. Everything that had been my identity for the past year was yanked out from beneath me. Everything came crashing down.

Just as with Susie Pearl in London, I was contributing so little to my friendship with Manuel, and expecting so much in return. *At any cost* was costing me the very partnerships and relationships that meant the most to me.

It didn't take much to see that Manuel had lost faith as well. However, my interpretation was that he lost faith in the business (delusional). In reality, he lost faith in our friendship. Our odyssey, a kindred business partnership and deep friendship, led to this crossroad.

I now realize that my careless attitude created a divide of indifference between myself and those in my inner circle. Manuel was merely the symbol of the beginning of the end of many of my relationships.

I thanked him for coming to help me. The silence as we moved boxes from the office on the third floor to my car was more deafening than reflective. I was angry that I couldn't save my business, and moving all of my desks and chairs into my apartment seemed like a hopeless option. The fact that Manuel was the only one to show up to help me compounded my frustration.

So this is how it feels to fall flat on your face.

It's extremely difficult to have any perspective on life experiences when we're right in the middle of them.

As Manuel and I drove in silence up to my house in Washington Heights, I considered all that we had been through together. All I wanted to do was talk, but really, there was nothing to say.

The silence was broken. My cell phone rang.

"Hello?" I said to the unknown number.

"Is this Jake Sasseville?" the caller asked.

"Yes it is, how can I help you?"

"My name is Eric Shutzer, from The Schutzer Group," he said.

I thought it might have been a TV network. My heart raced for a moment.

His voice was nasally, a stark similarity to the rat character Templeton in *Charlotte's Web*. I imagined he wore a bow tie from the sound of his voice.

"Mr. Sasseville, I'm calling to inform you that we've been retained by Carrie Barrett in a matter concerning her loan to you in the amount of $30,000."

The call was on speakerphone and Manuel looked over at me, clearly concerned.

What is this guy talking about?

"Are you familiar with this loan agreement, Mr. Sasseville?" Templeton asked.

I cleared my throat.

"Um, ahem, yeah. It was a loan for $40,000," I shot back, almost too honest for my own good.

The lawyer was ready for my response.

"Yes, but our client only has documentation for the $30,000," Templeton said.

That's true. The $10,000 that Carrie loaned me when I ran out of money in November was undocumented.

"Okay..." I let him speak.

Templeton explained that Carrie made numerous attempts to begin collecting on the two-year loan. I explained that I had responded to each of her emails, explaining that I would put the money together just as soon as I could, but that my business was in rough shape.

The irony here is that I had just packed up my office and was closing shop. Rough shape was an understatement.

Templeton said that wasn't good enough.

"She's expecting to receive the money within fourteen days. Otherwise we've been retained to pursue it by any and all means required by this firm in the State of New York."

Silence.

I almost crashed on the FDR Drive as my full attention was now on Templeton and not the road.

Whoops.

"I'll do the very best I can do sir," I said, defeated.

I started shaking uncontrollably. Carrie and I had exchanged several emails and she had hinted that she had a collection law firm she was speaking to. I assured her that I had every intention to pay her back and that I just didn't have the resources. I tried to negotiate a payment plan with her, which she immediately rejected.

In *The 48 Laws of Power* by Robert Greene, one of the examples of how to maintain power and influence is to make sure you strike your opponent fast and deliberately, without warning. Carrie did just that. Except, I thought she was on my side?

My life felt like it was falling apart. I was losing my friends, my business and I had no money saved anywhere. I couldn't imagine how to pay Carrie $30,000 in two weeks. As kind as Carrie was to me in the beginning with the loan, I imagined that she was equally a shrewd business woman.

I managed to safely navigate to 173rd Street and Fort Washington Avenue, the place I called home. Manuel and I started to unload the car. I was happy I had the distraction of emptying the car, but couldn't get Carrie out of my mind.

Manuel was very surprised by this development. He and Mo (Carrie's son) were also friends, and Manuel had met Carrie. I introduced Manuel to Mo. He understood the seriousness of repaying the loan back on time, but something about her actions, after previously being freely generous and supportive, didn't make sense to him. It didn't make sense to me either.

I moved six offices worth of stuff into my small bedroom. I had just moved into the apartment with two other flat mates and had no furniture. I had no money for it. I didn't even have a bed. I crammed boxes and 10 office chairs into my room, alongside huge white boards, tables and desks.

I didn't have the money for a storage unit, and besides, this was a temporary solution before I was back on my feet, right?

Manuel had indeed gotten lost in "Jake world." He was the only one left standing. I think it clicked for him that day. He was about to graduate from New York University. Time he should've been devoting to his own entrepreneurial ideas he instead spent getting lost in mine. I don't think he regretted it, but I could tell he was finished. He wanted more than I had to offer.

Manuel and I hugged goodbye, and he wished me luck. It was the last time I'd see or talk to him for a very long time.

No distractions

I spent the next few months in my bedroom and exploring my new neighborhood. I remained persistent and consistent, pitching advertisers and networks daily. I checked in with my manager weekly, but nothing was developing on either coast. It was as if my career came to a screeching and abrupt halt, followed by an extensive standoff. The pain and defeat made it difficult to get up every morning and take showers, or even go outside.

But I did. I remained focused and as positive as possible.

In a matter of weeks I went from being an alternative late night star with the potential for millions of fans to being derailed and confined to a small 200 square foot bedroom, sleeping on an oversized beanbag and barely able to afford rent.

Even worse, I had lost all of my work friends and my best friend Manuel.

You see, *at any cost* became an omnipresent truth. The failure of the business was more than a monetary loss or slight pause on my rise to fame. The failure of my business triggered the need for a massive shift in my life.

23

BEING VULNERABLE

How my staff screamed at me in the streets of New York, and even though failure's a bitch, owing people money is even worse.

People seldom do what they believe in. They do what is convenient, then repent.

— BOB DYLAN

My roommates, Mokay and Mike, thought I was crazy for sleeping on a beanbag. It never occurred to me that my living situation was sub-optimal. I was in the middle of a devastating moment in my life, and it didn't quite seem as ridiculous as it does in hindsight.

My emotional state straddled between depressed and hopeful. I sat for days, making calls and getting none returned, believing that somehow this would work out.

None of it materialized.

Some things aren't meant be. It sounds cliché, but once you learn that not everything happens as you like for it to, even with the best of intentions, this can release a lot of resistance and frustration.

I was nowhere near releasing any frustration. I was damn angry and scared as hell as I watched everything around me evaporate. My phone just stopped ringing. Emails went from several hundred a day to less than a dozen. Still, I wanted to prove to the world that I could turn this around.

I got lost in my own narrative. The *anything it takes* version of Jake now became *do whatever it takes to turn it around and make good.*

The only time my phone rang was with angry staffers, demanding compensation.

"I don't know when, but I won't stop until I figure this out," I explained to each staff member in succession.

I had no other choice but to remain convinced. Each person was owned anywhere from $800 to $20,000. I answered every angry email and phone call, even if they just wanted to let off steam. I took responsibility for what I had done.

It was the least I could do for them. After all, much of my young team were weeks (if not months) behind on their personal bills because of the situation I caused. I felt deep sorrow for what I put them through, and not being able to fix it instantly was debilitating for me personally.

After three months of doing the same thing every day, hoping for an answer but finding none, I realized I had no plan. If you think my staff was pissed, consider what Ford Motor Company thought of their plan-less pioneer.

"Jake, this is absolutely unacceptable," said Jen Wells at Ford's advertising agency, JWT, who months prior was becoming a best friend. "What is your plan to fix this?"

Again, I had no plan.

"We thought you had the airtime already purchased on ABC when you pitched us," she said, irate. "We went to our client with this information knowing there would be challenges, but never expected that you would get taken off the air!"

Learning the importance of communication around contract details is baptism by fire.

For the record, I never said that the time on ABC after *Kimmel* was paid for in advance. I said it had been secured with contracts (which was true), but never that I had paid it in advance. However, my ambiguity infuriated Ford. This taught me how what you don't say is just as important as what you do say.

Semantics aside, I needed to get back to the grind.

I devised a plan that made the show appear attractive to potential new buyers. Instead of saying that I was re-launching *The Edge*, I instead framed the opportunity for advertisers as *The Edge's* "season two," boasting strong ratings and great PR from season one.

As I reflected on my "first season," and thought about how to present my story in a way that didn't show failure, but instead advancement, this idea of distinguishing season one versus season two seemed to feel good. I couldn't acknowledge the failure at that moment. It was too painful. Spinning it as a "second season" gave me relief. No one needed to know that season one was only five episodes. Television was changing. Some shows have eight-episode seasons, other have twenty-two episodes in a single season.

New people I pitched didn't know the difference. As long as I could contain the damage done to Ford and Overstock, and none of my team went public or sued me, then I could craft a compelling story for new brand partnerships.

An unexpected lesson on how to be vulnerable

I was lucky to have the support of Mike and Mokay, the two guys I lived with. I didn't know either of them very well before we lived together. I knew Mokay was from Sierra Leone but grew up in London. He worked in pharmaceutical sales. His love for life is infectious and he became an older brother to me.

Mike, a Dublin-born musician, is one of the kindest hearted people I know. They were both five years older than me. We moved in together in April, and I moved out of my office in April. I didn't tell them anything about my predicament because I was ashamed.

When we moved in together, we decided that I would be responsible for collecting rent checks and paying the $2,350 monthly rent to the landlord.

A few months into our new living situation, desperately and foolishly, I kept some of the money and didn't pay the full rent.

Mike and Mokay eventually found out about my transgressions (thanks to two eviction notices in our mailbox – whoopsies). I felt like the kid who was caught stealing gum at the grocery store.

Mokay was more visibly frustrated with me than Mike. We had a consultation in the living room. They were both concerned about their money and our credit with the landlord, but equally with my well-being.

I kept so much inside. All at once, it came out. I told them everything. I cried unstoppably. It hurt so much to say it out loud, to verbalize that I couldn't save my business, to talk about the hurt and disappointment I caused to the people I cared about most. I told them I lost everything. My dreams, my finances, my relationships – they had all been shattered in a matter of a few months.

They listened empathetically; both Mokay and Mike were visibly moved by my admissions. They didn't get angry. I felt the weight of bricks lift off my heart, chest and shoulders as I admitted my failure for the first time out loud.

I apologized for not paying the rent and explained that I'd figure out a way to pay it in full.

In the face of a possible eviction, Mike and Mokay hugged me and loved me. They accepted me for the wholeness of who I am, not just for the good qualities. They accepted this very dark side of me. There is no more liberating moment in one's life than being accepted. No one had ever loved me this way before.

I've always taken care of myself. Since I left for France when I was 15, I've been on my own. I've had a ton of help, but no one has taken care of me. I had never allowed myself to be vulnerable. And yet, that day with Mike and Mokay changed me. It taught me that my shortcomings are loveable. And that honesty is essential.

At a time when I felt myself hardening inside, the unconditional love of Mike and Mokay gave me courage to move forward. The sky became bluer. Water tasted better. Plants smelled fresher. Life felt worth living, and turning my business around seemed not only possible, but inevitable.

Screaming drive-by

Speaking of vulnerability, a week later I was having pizza at a local pizza joint in Queens. Cheese was dripping out of my mouth. One of my former cameramen (who was owed about $5,000) passed by the pizza shop in the backseat of a cab and spotted me sitting at the window.

We made eye contact before he yelled.

"Sass-e-ville!" he shouted. "When the fuck am I going to get my money?"

His voice trailed off as the cab sped away. He scared the shit out of me, and it was clear that frustration was turning into anger.

Later that afternoon, Lori Fitch called me. She remained hopeful and was trying to support me as best as he could.

"Jake, it's Lori,. How's it going?" Lori asked.

"I'm fine, I guess. Thanks for calling," I said.

"I don't know what you're doing for cash, but maybe you can get a part-time job," Lori offered. "I heard they have good benefits at Starbucks."

I was grateful for her thoughts, but enraged by her suggestion.

I will not become a barista. Failure is not an option. Becoming a barista would force me to take my eye off the prize.

Father and son

After my call with Lori , I phoned my dad, frustrated at my situation. I loved and respected his ideas and advice very much. Every friend who has ever met my dad acknowledges his humor and his profound sense of empathy and love.

My dad told me a story about his early 20s when he was accepted into American University. He was married to my mom and on the fast track to joining the Peace Corps and working in intelligence in Washington D.C.

But he reasoned that D.C. would be too expensive, and because my mom was concerned about the Peace Corps, he opted to not leave for The Solomon Islands in the South Pacific.

He chose not to do any of it, and rationalized it to protect himself. So instead of traveling the world and following his dream, my dad ended up as a post-grad tollbooth collector on the Maine Turnpike, making $8 per hour. As my dad put it, he *blinked*.

My dad's life – the wholeness of it, not just one part – is his gift to me that keeps giving. In my moment of despair and failure, I had a decision to make. Was I going to blink, or was I going to press on no matter what?

My dad went on to have two kids (my brother and me) and eventually found happiness raising us, having various careers in the nursing home business, as a teacher, a social worker and later, a life coach. He has contributed to the well-being of thousands of people in his career. Even still, I think he wonders what *could* have been had he not blinked.

My dad visited the set of my new TV show, *Delusions of Grandeur*, in Chicago recently. We took this picture together. He didn't believe me when I said I showed up at the office in PJs and robes.

You get the answers to the questions you ask. Everytime.

"How can I go bankrupt?" yielded certain answers, even if just in my head.

"How can I find a way to focus on my business and turn it around no matter what – and have fun in the process?" gives an entirely different answer.

Be focused and deliberate on the questions you're asking yourself. You will get the answers.

Many, many people disagreed vehemently with me. That is okay. I've seen it work time and again for others and myself.

As I started re-focusing on the questions I asked myself, I indeed got a different answer. That answer came in the form of my brand new Ford Focus 2008 with less than three thousand miles on the odometer that Ford gifted to me six months before.

After two Facebook posts and one test-drive, my Ford Focus sold for $15,000 to a Massachusetts woman. I paid my debt to some of the ABC stations and put the rest in a bank account.

I called Susie in London.

"Susie, I'm feeling so down," I told her. She knew about the collapse of my company.

"You're more than invited to come here to our little home to be re-energized," Susie Pearl offered.

Her "little home" was a grand sprawling estate in the southeast corridor of London, in the county of Kent.

I thought about my financial situation for a moment.

"I'll think about that," I said, before hanging up the phone.

I called her back two minutes later to accept her invitation.

I was on a plane to London the next week.

24

BEING DETACHED

Focus on what feels good, even if that means moving to London indefinitely and taking your foot off the gas momentarily

'All the art of living lies in a fine mingling of letting go and holding on.'

— HAVELOCK ELLIS

It was July 2008 and I just purchased a one-way ticket to London.

Susie moved from the bustling London celeb-and-posh area of Chiswick and to Southeast England, in the county of Kent. Paul McCartney is her neighbor. His daughter and Susie Pearl's son attend classes together.

The picturesque English countryside was rejuvenating. Susie Pearl brought me to lunch the first day I arrived and reminded me how much she loved me. Her deeds spoke volumes. We laughed for hours over lunch.

I settled into my cabin above the garage on Susie Pearl's ten acre estate. Outside my front door was everything I could dream of. The house was an old 1900s beer factory, called an Oast House. The grounds were graced with a heated swimming pool, acres of gardens with a variety of flowers and trees prime for deep meditations, and also boasted trampolines and a tennis court.

"How long can I stay?" I asked, mere hours after I arrived.

"Jakey, I don't give a damn." Susie responded, running from one room to the next. "Stay as long as you need. You'll be in the cabin. You can celebrate Christmas in there for all I care."

We laughed.

Susie said whatever I found in the fridge was mine to eat. I was invited to spend as much or as little time with her and her family as I wished. Susie Pearl has never ceased to amaze me with her generosity and love.

Susie Pearl's young son Will, now 9, leaped with boundless energy at the sight of me. I was just a kid in a 20-something year old's body after all. Every afternoon when he got home from school, Will b-lined straight to the cabin, and pulled me out of whatever I was doing to jump around on the trampoline.

I had so much fun. I felt such relief and joy for the first time in a long time.

I explored the libraries in the main house. I found books on life, love and starting over. I read all of them. I practiced meditation several times a day. I'd go for runs in the forest, and sing The Beatles at the top of my lungs (hoping Sir Paul would come out and harmonize *Yellow Submarine* with me).

I was beginning to put my failures into perspective. I had to put them behind me. I had to be in a good state of mind in order to start over again, and I couldn't do that if I continued dwell on the past.

Once I started to feel like myself again, I made a call to Martin Baker and Pete Coogan, veteran TV producers that worked for Disney in London. I asked if they wanted to produce *The Edge UK* with me, just for fun. Shockingly, they accepted and asked that we first do a pilot. They agreed to finance it.

Maybe I can make it in the UK before I make it in America.

Within a month of the pilot being wrapped, we had meetings scheduled with MTV Europe, BBC and ITV. I didn't care what happened at the meetings. I just wanted to have fun and remind myself of what it felt like to feel good and to be creative in the television industry.

All the networks were receptive. Some spent several meetings discussing how "Jake" might work in the European market. In the end, no one bit. But it sure was fun considering the possibilities.

Sometimes things take a long breath or two (or two thousand) before you can make them right. After going against the grain for months, I had to let go. I had to shift my focus if I was going to remain sane. I'm of no use to anyone if I'm not in a good state of mind, including myself.

I came to grips with the fact that I may never do television again. I learned detachment was not about giving up, but about being okay with whatever happened. And through meditation and a deep desire to move myself into a better-feeling state, I became okay again.

Television was a piece of the wholeness of what I am, not *the* whole thing. It was a tough lesson at the age of 22.

Not everyone will understand your process

Once word spread amongst former staff members that I was living in Europe, the hostilities ensued. My inbox filled with a-million-and-one tirades—laced with choice words—demanding inked checks.

Reclaiming my sense of self was not going to put money in their accounts, they asserted. I answered each note, and told them I was working as hard as I could to get them paid. Indeed I was. In between trampolines and doing a pilot, I was making calls every day via Skype to pitch brands.

Some mistook my desire to take care of myself for carelessness, pissing them off. They called it selfish.

Once you let someone else dictate how they want you to respond, you've misplaced your own guidance system for someone else's. I knew I had to find a way to replenish myself in order to do right by anyone. Focus on what feels good. Everything else will flow effortlessly.

Whether you're employed, an aspiring entrepreneur or living on welfare, you don't need to explain your decisions to anyone. Find a place of well-being in your reality and turn your focus toward it fully.

The ah-hah moments come unexpectedly

After several weeks of meditations and bouncy afternoons on the trampoline, I recognized I still wanted to be on TV and I couldn't stop being an entrepreneur. Being an entrepreneur is woven into the fabric of my being and there was nowhere else to go besides forward. I committed myself to figuring out a way to turn the ship around. I had a stronger sense of self than ever before and felt rested, balanced and determined.

I had none of the answers, but my new intention was set. I'd find a way to get back on television and play the game, but I'd do so sustainably with love and respect for the people that would put me there.

25

BEING ACCOUNTABLE

Hindsight is 20/20, even with white-collar crimes

Nothing is more sad than the death of an illusion.

— ARTHUR KOESTLER

While I was reading a new book by Lester Levinson in the cabin in England, a friend of mine from America Skyped in.

My friend said he had something important to tell me. It was about our mutual friend Mo Barrett, my pal in New York who's mom Carrie was the first to invest in the company (and helped me save it). Carrie worked for the biggest rock band in the world in Ireland.

Mo wasn't in my life much anymore. We drifted apart and I finally accepted that people come and go. If they go quickly, they usually come in to teach important lessons. I'm forever grateful to Mo for all that he taught me about life. He helped me re-wire and re-boot an old system of thinking and it changed my life.

My friend on Skype, however, delivered a blow to the gut.

"Jake, you need to hear this," he began. "It's Carrie, Mo's mom. She was just arrested in Ireland."

"Why? What happened?"

"I don't know, but I'm reading online that she's been accused of embezzling a lot of money."

What the fuck?

"Whaddya mean dude?" I stuttered. "Are you sure?"

"You should read some of these articles online," he suggested. "Maybe you want to tell your financial people too."

This can't possibly be real. Carrie was just hounding me for the $30,000 I borrowed.

In fact, I just received this letter from Eric Schutzer, Carrie Barrett's collection attorney in New York.

Subject: Carrie Barrett loan
Dear Mr. Sasseville,

As my previous correspondence informed you, this firm now represents Carrie Barrett with regard to your outstanding loan. Further communications sent directly to Carrie Barrett are strictly forbidden.

In response toyour recent email, see below, I am writing to inform you that unless payment in full of $30,000.00 is received by this office immediately, this office has been authorized to proceed with legal action against you. Asmentioned in our previous correspondence, if litigation is initiated our client will petition the court to hold you responsible for her court fees, attorney fees and interest charges, in addition to, the full amount of the loan.

The loan agreement which you signed was for $30,000.00 and my client's records only reflect lending you $30,000.00. Although my client will make no objection to your paying $40,000.00, if you wish, the amount necessary to satisfy the loan and resolve this matter is $30,000.00.

Regarding your ability to repay the loan, I would suggest that you investigate all possible resources at your disposal to find the funds necessary to repay my client in full before litigation is initiated.
Regards,
Eric Schutzer

I quickly put two and two together. To my astonishment, based on what I read online and the uncharacteristic aggressiveness of Carrie, it became clear that she was trying to recover the money I owed her before she was arrested. The articles noted that an investigation had been proceeding for months, and that in fact, the infamous rock band she was working for terminated Carrie weeks ago.

The online sources claimed that Carrie Barrett embezzled millions of dollars from the bank account of the band, all in small amounts, over the course 2004-2008. The allegations were shocking. Carrie is now being charged with 181 counts of Theft and Fraud in Irish Court.

The articles cited that the money had been spent on lavish trips worth hundreds of thousands of dollars, an apartment in New York, expensive dinners, film school for Mo and other high priced items at Tiffany's and Sacks.

Whoa. Mo gifted me a one thousand dollar Tiffany bracelet years ago.

I grew weary of the accusations, wondering how a woman who's family I cherished and love was capable of such abhorrent behavior. I didn't want to believe the articles, but equally, everything finally made so much sense.

The money. The trips. The food. The apartment. The limitless spending account. The attempt to collect the debt so suddenly. The lawsuit threats.

I think people do some very bad things. But I don't think that makes them bad people. I don't defend what Carrie Barrett is accused of doing. If it's true, she should be punished for it. However, I also don't think that what she did makes the lessons she taught me any less significant.

At the time of the eighth round of edits of this book (August 2012), Carrie Barrett has been sentenced to seven years in prison after being charged with 181 counts of Theft for stealing $3.5 million.

How can you do this to one of the most high profile bands in the world and think you're not going to get caught?

At any cost seemed to be toxic. I nearly lost everything – I lost friendships, burned my business to the ground, pissed off my closest allies like

Ford and Overstock.com, and now I realized that the money that I started it all with wasn't clean.

I started to set new goals for myself. I set intentions of working hard and creating *sustainability* and *authenticity* within my work. If I was going to play ball again, this would have to be my new ethos.

26

BEING UNMISTAKABLY LOUD

Breaking Rules To Break Back In To The Biz

I realized that kids everywhere go for the same stuff; and seeing as we'd done it in England, there's no reason why we couldn't do it in America too.

— JOHN LENNON

After several months of reflection and growth in England, I returned to the U.S., grateful to Susie Pearl, her family and her friends for reigniting and inspiring me to move forward.

I decided business as usual wouldn't work. My success was too far behind me. I needed to create a new story and make a big impact to get advertisers back on board with the second season of *The Edge.*

Calling brands and agencies for new business was only half of the battle. Brands with big money get thousands of calls a month. I needed to stand out. You have to figure out a way to stand out, too. Living small doesn't do you or anyone else around you justice. In fact, living largely subconsciously gives others permission to live large as well.

I decided to start doing stunts to get the attention of brands and press – really big stunts – stunts that would capture the imagination of my public.

PART 1:

WENDY'S

———◆———

A quiet return to the United States turns into a corporate brawl and a broken world record

I pitched to Wendy's ad agency while I was still in England, but nothing happened. Many deals get lost in the perpetual state of ambiguity, where decision makers don't say *NO* but they don't say *YES* either. It's enough to drive a restless entrepreneur (even more) insane.

The last conversation I had with the agency went something like this.

Exec: "Is your TV show on the air in 85% of the country?"
Jake: "No, I anticipate I'll be in 40% by next year."
Exec: "Are you on TV right now?"
Jake: "I'm on hiatus. Season two starts later this year."
Exec: "Let's talk in two weeks."

This was followed by weeks of silence. Frustrating, right?

I called the Vice President of Marketing at Wendy's headquarters in Columbus, Ohio and left a great message.

No return call.

Keep in mind I had no clue how many households I'd be in for "season 2." I knew I had to figure out a different business model to get back on TV because paying my way on air on ABC wouldn't be an option. However, those were details for another day. My job was to make enough noise to open the door to have the conversations with the people in charge who matter most.

Hearing the word NO was a way of life for me. I trained my mind to hear it, accept it, and consider that it's only one step closer to the word YES. You must do the same. Train your mind.

You can't hide from Google search results. One entry of the name 'Jake Sasseville' and the great big gap between "Jake after Jimmy" to "Present day" might ruin everything.

I had to make some noise. Not too much, but just enough to re-frame the conversation from "Who is Jake Sasseville?" to "This guy is very interesting…"

It's a delicate balance between full-out stalking people and giving them the space they deserve to make decisions.

Simple marketing to stage a comeback

Jake Bronstein, a genius marketer, is responsible for the million-dollar business "Bucky Balls" (Google it), "Tap'd Water" (local tap water packaged and sold locally to parched environmentalists) and social media campaigns behind Richard Linklater's films. I like Jake's ability to think quickly with a sense of effortlessness.

I rang him and asked for his help.

"Jakey baby," I said. "I need to get Wendy's on my side. They're giving me the cold shoulder."

Jake Bronstein knew my reputation for shaking down people to get their attention. He knew no idea was too outrageous, and chances are, I'd immediately jump on one if I liked it.

"Break a world record for the most women to have lunch with you at a Wendy's."

YES.

"Hell, I'll make a requirement that they all be named "Wendy!"

"Good one, dude," Jake Bronstein said. "Let me know how I can help."

It was a five-minute call. I knew exactly what needed to be done. I had to break a world record for the most amount of women named Wendy having lunch with me at a Wendy's. And I had to do it in Wendy's backyard in Columbus, Ohio.

I called my virtual assistant, Afaq Tariq, in Karachi, Pakistan. He was a 22-year-old student who worked at Timesvr, the virtual assisting company. I paid $4 an hour for his services and his work was stellar.

"Afaq," I said. "I need you to log into my Facebook page and create a World Record Breaking Attempt fan page."

"No problem Mr. Jake," Afaq said. "What else?"

"I need you to search for all women named Wendy within 100 miles of Columbus, Ohio," I said.

I could hear Afaq typing.

"I'll send you an email with the details, but the event is happening October 1st, cool?"

"But Mr. Jake, that's just two weeks away."

"Yes, I know Afaq. We're going to need to move quickly. Send all the women named Wendy personal Facebook messages."

Afaq was off. He worked through the night so I'd have the results by morning in New York.

(I highly suggest outsourcing certain tasks to virtual assistants.)

Within a day of the call with Jake Bronstein, dozens of women named Wendy began accepting our invitation. I hadn't cleared it with the Wendy's restaurant or any of the executives at Wendy's corporate. It was going to be grassroots and sudden. Take the opponent by surprise and turn them into an ally (at least that was the plan).

I called Jake Bronstein and asked him to invite his friends at Guinness World Records and The Universal Record Database to Columbus.

"Jake, one other thing," I said. "Are you in for joining me in Columbus in two weeks?"

"I wouldn't miss this for anything," Jake Bronstein chuckled.

I bought plane tickets and made it official. It was the last few hundred dollars I had in my checking account. Balls out.

Maybe you're thinking how sudden and sporadic all of this seems. Yes, it was, but what should I wait for? I had a simple idea and I was excited to make it happen. The real question is, why are you waiting for tomorrow to get started on *your* idea today?

Only Afaq Tariq, Jake Bronstein, myself, and a handful of women named Wendy in Columbus knew about the event. The secrecy was intentional. If onlookers can't figure you out, they can't stop you either. Journalists love to write about this. Be smart and move quickly. Don't let the competition know what's happening. It's more fun for everyone.

I have nothing to lose and everything to gain.

Afaq got Accepted Invitation notes from over one hundred women named Wendy to have lunch with me at Wendy's in Columbus.

Wind the press machine up.

I made some strategic moves to seed the story to the press five days before blast off.

I called my friend Rainn Wilson, star of *The Office* on NBC. I had never asked him for a favor quite like this before, but I needed all the help I could get.

"Rainn," I said. "You have 3,000,000 Twitter followers. Would you mind tweeting about this absurdly hilarious world record-breaking stunt I'm doing in Columbus?"

"Sure, when do you want the tweet to go out?" Rainn said, without hesitation.

"Let's say early morning October 1st," I suggested.

"Deal, just send me what you want it to say," Rainn said.

Locked and loaded.

Next, our team reached out to local news sources in Columbus.

They love to do news stories on shit like this.

Within a few hours of pitching the story, we got questions like "Why?", "Who are you?" and "Why would you do this here if you're from New York?"

Sometimes a direct question deserves a vaguely honest answer.

"We're doing this because we want to remind people how easy it is to have fun," I'd say.

We didn't want the press know that this was in an attempt to get new business from Wendy's.

Let the story unfold and let people find out the crucial details on their own.

Many in the media thought this was a fake publicity stunt.

"This is very real," I'd reassure reporters. "I'm going to Columbus with my cameras October 1st. We'll see you there."

Midwest as a launching pad

The last time I was this nervous flying to the Midwest, it was on the day before my "Jake after Jimmy" stunt with Manuel at St. Louis University. Folks in the midwest seem to dig the vibe of what we do. I love their support.

Still, I was terrified that no one would show up.

What would Wendy's think?

We landed at 10:00 a.m. and Rainn Wilson tweeted out to 3,000,000 people while we were in the air:

"My good friend Jake Sasseville is crazy. Breaking world record for most women named Wendy having lunch with him at Wendy's."

He gave the link.

Perfect!

Jake Bronstein and I were picked up by our local Columbus coordinator, Leslie. Leslie told us she was watching the Wendy Williams talk show that morning and that Wendy was talking about our Wendy's Record Breaking attempt.

Fuck ya!

We arrived at an empty Wendy's parking lot at 11:00 a.m. Call-time was noon for our mid-western ladies named Wendy.

Jake Bronstein stayed in the car with Leslie at first, and I paced the parking lot.

I was nervous. At 11:30 a.m. the World Record Breaking officials arrived.

A woman approached us.

"Is this where the record breaking thing is happening?"

"You must be Wendy," I greeted.

We had big name tags that said: "HI, MY NAME IS WENDY."

We plastered it to her chest. She had no choice.

News crews from NBC and CBS parked their vans and were setting up to cover the event.

We were getting closer to noon.

Maybe this silly idea will work.

Just then, half a dozen women named Wendy showed up in unison, as if they carpooled to the parking lot together.

"We're all Wendy's," they said, smiling. "And we're ready for our lunch!"

I was ecstatic.

They cackled.

The other Jake (Bronstein) helped distribute nametags.

Just as I was being interviewed by *Columbus Underground*, a local entertainment daily newspaper in Columbus, the manager of the Wendy's store we were about to infiltrate interrupted me.

(Keep in mind, this was the Wendy's restaurant down the street from Wendy's corporate headquarters, and we told <u>no one</u> that we were coming).

"Sir, excuse me, can I speak with you for a moment," the manager asked me.

We stepped aside from the crowd.

"We know what you're about to do here, we heard about it on the radio this morning."

"Really?" I said.

I acted surprised, the ignorant ringleader to my own circus.

"Yes, everyone in town has heard something. We just want to let you know how grateful we are that you chose our store."

OMG!

He was grateful that I chose *his* store. This was better than being read the Riot Act, which is what I was expecting.

"In fact, I'd like to offer lunch on me today" the owner of the store offered, "for you, and for however many women named Wendy show up."

I thanked him and gave him a hug. "This is going to be great," I reassured him.

When I turned my back, we were up to what looked like 40 hungry women named Wendy.

News reporters were fawning over the local Wendy celebrities, talking to them about how they found out about the idea and why they showed up.

We created this out of nothing. POOF.

At about 12:05 p.m., I paraded the pack of women into Wendy's for their free lunch.

Single file, the line stretched around the restaurant. The record breaking official stood at the cash register, verifying a head count.

The people already enjoying lunch in the restaurant were aghast. The buzz filled the air.

People found genuine excitement in the novelty of our record-breaking attempt.

Fun for fun's sake.

Somehow, these Midwestern housewives who had never met each other felt like they were a part of something exciting. I played temporary Wendy's host to my new female friends, visiting each table throughout the afternoon.

The media continued to interview the women when I noticed three people in suits staring at me from the corner of the restaurant.

They don't look happy.

"Hi, I'm Jake. Are you here for the Wendy's event?" I asked, extending my hand.

"We're from Wendy's corporate, Jake," the woman said. I recognized her voice. I had spoken to her on the phone weeks before.

"What do you think you're doing here?" she continued.

"Having fun," I said casually.

She asked what gave me the idea that this was okay.

"I'm paying for this on my own," I returned, with a smile. "You won't get a bill from me, don't worry."

Sometimes dealing with controversy head on is easier. Choose your battles, own your genius and never back down when you're right.

In reality, the marketing exec should be thrilled that people were talking about Wendy's all across the country right now.

Moments later, as the executives huddled in the corner and I was being interviewed by the local NBC affiliate, the door swung open.

The cameraman panned away from me and focused on the middle-aged woman who entered the store.

I was confused.

The room got silent.

A short, five-foot-eight ginger headed woman walked in the store with a friend.

"Jake, you did it," someone whispered in my ear. *"That's* Wendy."

"Wendy, Wendy?"

I didn't understand.

"Yes, Wendy," the person nudged, "The REAL WENDY."

Dave Thomas' daughter?

"Wendy's was named after her," Leslie said. "She's the daughter of the founder of Wendy's."

Whoa. The heiress of the Wendy's fortune just walked into my little event. Shit just got real.

She made eye contact with me and slowly approached. I thought she was pissed. I broke out in a sweat.

"Excuse me," she said softly. "Are you Jake Sasseville?"

"Yes I am, ma'am," I said, trying not to choke on my words.

"I just wanted to let you know that my father would have loved your energy for our brand if he were still alive," she told me. "You should be very proud of what you've created here today."

I grew up watching Dave Thomas in Wendy's commercials (and eating at Wendy's). I was stunned.

After a showdown with the executives and the ad agency back in New York City, I got a total confirmation from the heiress of Wendy's herself. It made it all worth it.

It wasn't about selling burgers that day. It wasn't even about winning new business or making money. It was about thinking differently, and acting on it. We were daring to show up in Ohio without asking permission. We stimulated some, and polarized others. We gave them reason to laugh and to think. We brought some love and light to Wendy's that day and had a great time doing it.

We managed to get a partial group shot of the women named Wendy. Jake Bronstein and I are toward the right.

Keep them guessing. Always.

It was time to make an announcement.

"Excuse me, everyone," I announced. "I am so appreciative that each of you showed up here to have some fun today."

The crowd applauded.

"Many have asked me why I chose to do this. Frankly, I didn't know why at the beginning either."

The crowd laughed, perhaps a self-reflection that they were nuts to accept a random invitation like this on Facebook.

"But I now realize it was to help us all remember how easy it is to have fun. As a token of my thanks, besides the burgers, I'd like to do something special for you."

Women looked at each other, curious.

"Air Tran Airways is a partner of ours and they have been kind enough to give me two free, first-class roundtrip airline tickets anywhere Air Tran flies."

"And I'm giving them away to one of you as my thanks."

The restaurant erupted with applause.

I love giving stuff away.

I filled a hat with the last names of each of the Wendy's, and had *the real Wendy* herself pick out the winning name.

"Wendy Bailey, you win!" I exclaimed.

The winning Wendy was sitting with three of her new friends. I caught a glimpse of her before the news cameras did and pointed them her way.

As I approached her to give her the tickets, she was crying profusely, clutching a bacon double cheeseburger.

I couldn't have pitched a better news story. I knew this would lead the newscast and that the bloggers covering the event would have a field day.

Wendy Bailey stood up and gave me a hug, telling me how grateful she was.

"This is a miracle!" Wendy said, over and over again. "I've been married for 22 years and have never had the money to go on a honeymoon!"

This woman is about to have the time of her life.

The room gave her a standing ovation. She uttered happily that she'd use the tickets to go to Montego Bay, Jamaica.

News crews jumped in for the interview. I stepped aside.

This is Wendy and her husband, on their honeymoon a few months later in Montego Bay.

"There's a lot more of where this came from if you'd find a way to make
this work," I said to the Wendy's execs, who were intrigued by the fanfair.

They thanked me for coming to Columbus.

We never did win the Wendy's business. In fact, all of their agencies
refused to continue speaking with me. They felt I had gone above their
heads and had disrupted their system. That's because I had.

From left to right, that's the Record Breaking
official, me, and on the other end of the sign, the *real*
Wendy Thomas (daughter of Wendy's founder Dave
Thomas) and Jake Bronstein in Columbus, Ohio.

'Business as usual' is dead.

If you don't want it bad enough, then step aside. There are enough people who do want it bad enough. If Wendy's didn't understand why I'm so valuable to their business, then they never would. Sometimes some business partnerships simply aren't meant to be.

If, by miracle, Wendy's had signed off on a deal, chances are they would have been a very difficult client to work with. As an entrepreneur, you have the right to fire clients (occasionally). Good relationships and synergy in business is key to sustainability.

If you love it, let it go.

I loved what we did at Wendy's. I loved what we created, and I especially loved seeing Wendy Bailey's honeymoon photos from Montego Bay. Just because Wendy's didn't say YES, doesn't mean anything was lost. Someone would surely say YES soon enough.

I felt it.

PART 2:

STATE FARM

———◆———

Why I felt justified to raise holy hell
in Bloomington, Illinois

State Farm Insurance was also on my list. From my research, they seemed earnest in wanting to talk with my generation in new ways with their advertising.

After calling the head of Public Relations at State Farm, I was introduced to their entertainment marketing agency, Davie-Brown, in Hollywood.

The "big idea" that we pitched State Farm was simple.

The State Farm Dude.

We'd create a branded character in late night TV, someone who would "always be there" and would boast exaggerated characteristics of a real-life State Farm agent.

Admittedly, this kind of kitschy product placement was something we used on my local access TV show, and it had paid the bills all the way to my ABC debut after Kimmel. It made us different and got people's attention.

I've never hid the fact that I paid my bills with brands like State Farm and, by fully owning it, it appeals to my audience. Suddenly, in a world where audiences say they don't like product placement, our audience consistently asked us for more.

After a few months of waiting for an answer, State Farm's entertainment agency Davie-Brown finally got back to us.

"While we appreciate you and your energy for our brand, this idea is not going to fit with our larger objectives," the representative said.

I couldn't resist the temptation to turn the NO into a YES.

Intuitively, I knew I had to push. Not immediately, but in another way. I had to create some magic. I had a new relationship with the advertising director at State Farm in Illinois. Though the agency said no, maybe I could get *his* attention.

My TV show was airing in State Farm's headquarters, Bloomington-Normal, Illinois. I sized up the local ABC affiliate (WHOI). It was a small TV station, but I found out it had a large morning show that all the State Farm execs watched. I plotted and planned my next move carefully.

I'd have to make big noise in State Farm's backyard in order to get people talking. But I must not piss them off.

I called the local morning show producer at WHOI News in Bloomington.

"Jessica," I said. "Hi. My name is Jake Sasseville calling from *The Edge*. *She didn't hang up the phone. That's a good sign.*

"I know this is a strange call, but *The Edge* airs on your ABC station after Kimmel," I explained. "We're on a short hiatus, but have some very exciting plans with State Farm."

None of this was a lie, yet important details were omitted. For example, our exciting plans with State Farm didn't yet get approved by State Farm.

It's very important to present a compelling story that is *relevant to the listener,* and not just appeal to your own self-interests. People think that reporters and journalists care about you. They don't. Give them a juicy story to bite into. Only then do *you* become interesting.

"I'm coming to Bloomington in the next few weeks," I said. "I'm going to meet with State Farm about an exciting new opportunity with *The Edge*."

Jessica asked some questions. She couldn't believe I was coming to Bloomington-Normal Illinois.

"I'd love to plan a segment where your morning news people interview me about our new campaign," I suggested.

"Well, what's your new campaign?" Jessica asked.

"It's called 'the State Farm Dude'," I said without hesitating.

"In fact," I went on, "we'd absolutely love to do a live casting on the morning news program to see if 'the State Farm Dude' might be cast in State Farm's backyard."

After several calls with Jessica, amazingly getting all of this approved with her management, I got on a plane with my television crew the following week and headed for Bloomington, Illinois.

State Farm had no idea I was coming to town.

What I proposed to Jessica is that we'd do segments in between news, weather and sports. I told her we'd bring in real people off the streets of

Central Illinois to sing the State Farm jingle and gush about why they'd be the perfect "State Farm dude."

Sometimes you're not going to get support for the things you want the most. People will look at you strangely. They may say no. Sometimes, selective honesty combined with massive action works.

Don't knock the hustle.

And don't be afraid of standing out. Slings and arrows aside, it's better than not standing out at all. Trust me. You want to be known, even if people don't always like you. Controversy sells. A good story is priceless.

I decided to email the advertising director at State Farm and say I was "just passing through town." Of course, this was a ridiculous email because no one passes through Central Illinois without reason.

I arrived at the studio in the middle of grasslands Illinois with a two-person crew. I used my guest spots on the morning news, in between weather and sports, to announce the official casting for "the State Farm Dude."

I announced the very campaign that State Farm and their advertising agencies shot down.

I had a feeling that someone from State Farm would be watching.

After the newscast, Mark Welp and Gretchen Wertz, the two news anchors on HOI Morning News, snapped a picture. Mark recently un-friended me on Facebook. I'll never know why.

Now that things were in motion, I had all day to kill in Illinois. I was due back at the studio the next morning, with people who would (hopefully) show up to be a part of the casting.

As I write about this story, now years older, I'm not sure I could muster up the courage to take on the establishment in the same ways I did when I was younger. This is why I ask students who are studying business or marketing in college, if they plan to go out in the "real world" and test their skills after graduation, why aren't they just doing it now? I got away with a lot just because of my age. You can too.

Plus, in today's crowded creative economy, you frankly can't afford not to stand out.

As I hit 'send' on the press release that afternoon, I simultaneously got an incoming call. The area code was 309. It was State Farm headquarters.

"Jake, just passing through, eh?" the advertising director of State Farm quipped.

I could tell the ad director, a 20-year veteran of the industry, was amused, curious and concerned, all at once. I've grown to love the people I do business with, but especially this advertising director at State Farm. Our tumultuous beginning was a

seed planted that required years of nurturing.

"Yes, sir. I love Illinois this time of year," I said.

(It was mid-July and humid as hell.)

"Well, why don't you come on in for a meeting with us," the advertising director suggested.

"I'd be happy to," I said. I tried to conceal my excitement, but I leaped into the air with joy.

He told me to meet him at 2:00 p.m. that afternoon.

Score.

After we were checked into the lobby of State Farm headquarters, a highly secure square of armored glass surrounding us, the advertising director met us and brought me to his office.

To my surprise, the meeting was smooth and friendly. Neither side showed their cards. I couldn't tell if the advertising director saw me on the morning show or if he saw the press release (I didn't send it to him) or if he was just responding to my "passing through Illinois" email.

I used every sales technique in the book. Initially, I pitched him a three hundred thousand dollar advertising deal. The ad director rolled his eyes, cueing me to lower the number so we could continue the conversation.

Was I a freewheeling 22-year-old with nothing to lose? Sure. But I was determined, believing deeply that *The Edge* was deserving of his ad money. Delusional or not, I didn't back down.

Like a good neighbor, he was extremely gracious. As we wrapped up the meeting, he sternly drew the line in the sand.

"You're not going to do anything stupid tomorrow are you, Jake?" the advertising director asked, revealing that he did indeed know about my plans with the "State Farm dude."

I froze for a second. He caught me off guard and he knew it.

"Nothing to upset you, friend," I returned.

The ad director was smarter than I gave him credit for. He knowingly brought me in for a meeting, took me under his wing and made sure I knew that he knew *exactly* what I was upto.

He killed me with kindness.

The next morning we went through with the State Farm auditions live on the morning news program.

"Like a good neighbor, State Farm is there."

Phones rang at the TV station. The local newspaper ran with the story and Inc. Magazine called me to do an interview. The shoe dropped and it finally was revealed that State Farm hadn't approved the gimmick.

SURPRISE.

The only person I didn't get a call from was the advertising director.

Articles about the event hit the newsstands and Internet within hours. Executives at State Farm were utterly confused, getting calls from the press and from their ad agency for comment. They had no comment, because they didn't know who authorized my arrival.

Before anyone could reach me and after I did the INC Magazine interview, I was on an Air Tran Airways flight back to New York City.

While I was in the air, Donna Fenn, contributing editor at INC Magazine, posted this story on INC:

Too Much Chutzpah?

How much chutzpah is too much chutzpah? Somehow, I doubt it's a question that Jake Sasseville has ever asked himself…

Now, he's set his sights on State Farmas a potential sponsor, but there's just one problem: the suits in Bloomington, IL are reluctant to open their hearts and their wallets. So how far do you go to land a piece of business?

"I don't like being told no, so I wanted to get in their back yard and gently bang on their door," says Sasseville.

So he went to Bloomington..., talked his way into co-hosting a local early morning show, HOI News Daybreak, and announced on air Tuesday that he was holding an open casting call for a new character on his show: State Farm Dude (or possibly Dudette). Think Rupert Jee on Letterman.

...So will Sasseville's antics pay off? Will State Farm Dude play a major role in season two of The Edge? Stay tuned.

This is me and Donna Fenn from INC Magazine at lunch recently. Even though she is one of my biggest skeptics, we are close friends, and our friendly disdain for each other has made for entertaining exchanges when we are booked to speak together at conferences and universities nationwide.

When I landed, my voicemail rang. I had missed several calls while in the air.

One of the voicemails was from the advertising director at State Farm. Shockingly, he wasn't upset. Instead, he expressed that he would've liked me to share with him that I was going to go to the press with the story. He could have alerted his team.

I acknowledged that I should have let him know, but I didn't want to stop the momentum by telling him.

In that short phone call, a guy I had only met one day before gained a lifetime of my loyalty and trust. I'd never try to hide anything from him again.

By contrast, the entertainment marketing agency, Davie-Brown, was livid.

"We told you no," the representative in Los Angeles yelled. "And you went behind our backs."

"You are not to reach out to our client any longer," a Davie-Brown rep said. "Do we understand each other?"

I was affable and agreed not to pitch any more business to State Farm. I didn't need to. Intuitively, I knew the work spoke for itself.

It took three years and a lot of time before State Farm would ever consider doing business with me. The first time they did, that same advertising director called, three years later, and offered to do a "test." That test started in 2010, and they have been consistent with their support of all my projects ever since.

I think secretly everyone at State Farm was entertained by the insanity of what we did. It was definitively absurd, although never malicious. I think that is a redeeming quality of our brand and our story. People can tell that even though I act almost without care of consequence, that I care deeply about them and their brand. It's a delicate balance that I don't always achieve.

You can't teach someone to like you, but you can remain persistent to find people that do. They are out there, and you will find them.

Some perspective on 'WHY?'

I saw my parents take very little risk when I was a child. I'm not sure they knew how to take risks. I wanted something more out of life than the constancy of the nine-to-five lifestyle. I think many in my generation feel the same.

The defining moment, though, of wanting *something more* out of my life was when I watched my baby brother die in my parents arm. He was thirteen years old.

He died of complications relating to a bone marrow transplant for acute myeloid leukemia.

On the day Alex died, the doctors told us he'd slowly stop breathing and that he wouldn't feel any pain thanks to the morphine. I was seventeen years old. It was a full twenty-four hours between when we were told Alex was going to die to when he actually did.

A long goodbye.

During the last few moments of Alex's life, my parents lay on either side of my brother's hospital bed. His eyes were closed and he had been unconscious for several hours. His breaths were fewer now, less than ten per minute. Our dog, Shadow, a beautiful black lab, spent the last night of Alex's life in the hospital room with us.

I stepped out of the room to get some ginger ale in the hallway. Most of that day is a blur, but not these final moments.

Not more than a few minutes later, I returned to the hospital room. My parents were alone with Alex, sobbing. My mom was softly grazing her hand through my brother's golden locks of hair, and my dad was kissing him gently on the cheek.

Alex was gone. He took his last breath while I was getting ginger ale. He died in my parent's arms as they lay in bed with him.

The sight of seeing my parents curled up next to my lifeless brother was excruciating and beautiful all at once.

They were there for his birth, and they held him as he died.

I watched Alex die, and it made me realize that not only do I want something more out of life than what others talked about, but I didn't want to wait for someone else to give it to me. Ever. This is the ethos I live by.

I got enough of a peak behind the curtain of life that day to remember that I never, ever want to live anything other than my most authentic life.

For all of my flaws and shortcomings, I hold this intention to what I do every day. And it's why I know that silly things like pissing off an ad agency is small peanuts compared to the magnitude of living one's life massively, and without apology.

PART 3:

COKE

Outsmart the Gatekeepers. Love and hate are the
opposite sides of the same coin.

Coca-Cola is represented by MediaVest advertising agency, one of the largest in the world. The Coca-Cola folks have known for me years. Unfortunately for them, they've always been hesitant when it comes to do business with me. They've kindly taken meetings and listened to me pitch, but none of the executives at MediaVest moved the ball beyond the initial conversations.

Common excuses included that I wasn't popular enough and that there wasn't enough money for Coke to spend. Coca-Cola, one of the largest advertisers in the world, telling me they didn't have enough money seemed like a sushi restaurant telling me they ran out of Yellowtail.

I wish instead of dodging me, Coke would come out and tell me the real reasons. Why is transparency so hard to find?

Over the course of years (yes, years!), I made presentations, listened to their feedback, tweaked my pitches, sent them gifts and tried many sales techniques. I couldn't get anyone within Coke's agencies to support me.

This isn't working. I need to try something different.

I did some research about new businesses Coke recently bought. Coke and Pepsi are known for buying smaller beverage companies and wrapping them into the larger portfolio, eliminating the competition and increasing profits.

I found out they had recently acquired Fuze Beverages for $250 million. I read how Lance Collins, founder of Fuze, started the fruity beverage company in his basement.

Quite a payday for a New Jersey basement fruit drink.

I called the advertising agency's executive who handled the entire Coca-Cola portfolio.

"Hey dude, I'd like to talk to you about Fuze," I said. "I haven't seen a lot of marketing for people my age and I think my audience will dig it."

His response was clear. They weren't interested in advertising on anything that I was involved with.

Fuck him.

I decided to take matters into my own hands with Fuze.

I asked my sales team to make a call to Fuze, by-passing the agency entirely (a no-no in the marketing world). I needed someone to buy into my vision.

I didn't tell the ad agency I was going behind their backs. I'd let them be surprised.

With my luck, and the skillful handiwork of Dave Philp, who is an all-American likeable sales dude who was working for me, we managed to get in front of the vice president of marketing and the director of public relations at Fuze's headquarters in New Jersey.

The meeting was light, full of laughter, and lots of ideating.

After two in-person meetings, the Fuze execs asked to see a proposal. We were thrilled.

Over the course of the next few weeks, we noodled through details of the deal. Dave Philp put together the proposal and led the conversations. I was so happy that he was able to maneuver the negotiations because he was the first guy I had hired in sales that actually was selling. Everyone else had a reason why they fell short. Dave was different and I told him how grateful and impressed I was.

Dave mentioned to me that I might want to consider alerting the ad agency that we were in the process of striking a six-figure deal with their client.

I made the choice not to tell the agency until the deal was done, for fear that they would become territorial and try to nix it.

I'm not suggesting you need to go behind people's backs to be successful. I am simply suggesting that business is a chess game, and that I will do anything to protect my King. I will sacrifice my Queen if I must.

As Steve Jobs frequently said, it's about making one good decision at a time. Not telling the agency, based on the information I had and the history with working (or not working) with Coke's ad agency, was the best decision.

Just as we were about to wrap up the contract, the Fuze VP called me personally.

"We'd like you to do a commercial for us that will debut in 26,000 movie theaters across the country in addition to our TV buy with you."

I was stunned. The marketing chief continued.

"To be honest, we've been unhappy with the creative work that our ad agency is doing. We think someone more connected to the grassroots can help us out. Are you willing to do this?"

I asked a lot of questions even though I knew I my answer was going to be YES. I wanted to know clarity, how it impacted the rest of the contract and if the agency would be involved. The cinema spot was going to be a 30-second introduction to the benefits of Fuze, with none other than Jake Sasseville starring in the commercial.

"We want to see creative ideas from you right now, not the agency."

I had a feeling that would piss off a lot of people, but cheerfully agreed to have my team put ideas together. The commercial spot, we were told, would receive 90 million impressions.

"I just want to let you know in full transparency," I began, "that I have pitched your agency for years, and I even called them about Fuze."

The marketing chief listened.

"They passed on me consistently, and I just don't want this to get awkward."

"No problem, we'll take care of the agency," she said.

Sweet!

The financial arrangement we made with Fuze for the package deal wasn't in my favor. Fuze execs saw how eager I was to do the deal, so they took advantage of the excitement. Still, even though it was only half of what I could've charged, it was a decent six-figure deal that would jump start my company, nearly thirteen months after I was taken off the air after Kimmel on ABC.

Just a few days before the national cinema spot, I got a call from Coca-Cola's ad agency. They asked me to come into their Times Square offices.

I brought my agent and my head of sales to the meeting. MediaVest expressed their disappointment with what I had done. I listened and acknowledged that I could have looped them into the conversation, but that I was concerned that they'd have cancelled the deal. I was honest and they were polite. It was clear that by the end of the meeting they weren't fans of me or my style of business.

And I was okay with that.

If everyone likes you, then no one loves you.

Turns out, my partnership with Fuze would be one of my most successful ever. The cinema spot was so popular that they extended the run from four weeks to six weeks in 26,000 movie theaters nationwide.

I was being recognized on the street and this was just the gusto I needed for a re-launch of *The Edge*. I was very proud of the partnership and of my team for grabbing the opportunity.

Still, even today, Mediavest refuse to do business with me. They've even instructed everyone in marketing at Coca-Cola headquarters in Atlanta to not take calls or answer emails from Jake Sasseville.

And I don't blame them. They see me as a threat.

Eventually they'll come around to me, like everyone does, and until then, I fully embrace that not everyone will be a fan. As Dr. Wayne Dyer reminds me,

"What other people think of me is none of my business. One of the highest places you can get is being independent of the good opinions of other people."

Being independent of others' opinions is something I struggle with daily, even though it seems like I really don't care.

PART 4:

DENNY'S

When they say NO, say HI… to their boss

At around the same time as Coca-Cola's ad agency passed and Fuze said yes, I was gearing up for activating a Denny's deal worth several hundred thousand dollars that I inked several months before.

It was perfect because with the money I secured from Fuze and the Denny's commitment, I'd re-launch my show stronger than ever.

In November, the same month I secured the Fuze deal, I got a call from Nicole Ryan, a vice president at Optimedia Agency, Denny's agency of record.

"Jake, it's Nicole," she said.

"Hiya, love," I said.

Nicole was my age, freshly out of college and had recently been given a ton of responsibility at the ad agency for negotiating several million in contracts with broadcast networks nationwide. She is a killer negotiator and I'm a huge fan.

"I have some bad news for you," Nicole said, her voice dropping. "Denny's is not going to be able to do the deal with you this year."

My mouth dropped.

"We have to use the money elsewhere. Our budgets have been slashed and we have to focus on the bigger buys. You're just too small."

I needed a certain amount of money in my bank account before I could deliver on the Fuze deal. Denny's cancelling meant the Fuze deal was now in jeopardy.

Shit.

"Is there any way we can turn this around?" I muttered, still in shock, reeling from the news, seeking solutions.

"We've tried everything with these budgets and numbers to keep you in," Nicole shared. "But we can't do this."

Nicole obviously felt terrible, but we both understood this was business.

As I listened to Nicole explain how Denny's was pulling the rug out from underneath me, I couldn't help but think over and over, *Denny's IS spending millions of dollars next year, it's just not on me… Yet.*

Therefore, the challenge was not that Denny's wasn't spending money, it's that I hadn't given them a good enough reason yet to spend it on me.

The conversation with Nicole went nowhere even though I tried to change her mind. I thanked her and hung up.

I meditated that afternoon. I didn't want to tell anyone on my team this news until I found a way to feel better about it first. Thanksgiving was around the corner.

After meditating for the afternoon and taking a hot shower, something inspired me to do some research on Denny's.

I found out that the Chief Marketing Officer for Denny's was a guy named Mark Chmiel. I loved what I read about Mark and how he understood the millennial generation and how to target them.

His career was almost exclusively in the restaurant business, an incredibly high risk and entrepreneurial industry. I thought Mark would connect with my story as a young entrepreneur in television.

I found Mark's phone number and called his office. No answer. I left a message. I found his email address and fired off the following:

Subject: Denny's and Jake
Date: November 2008

Hi Mark,

While you and I don't know each other formally, I have been working with your buying and planning teams at Optimedia.

I'm 22 years old and I'm executive producing and hosting THE EDGE WITH JAKE SASSEVILLE on ABC affiliates after Kimmel ("Jake after Jimmy").

After having the Denny's deal secured since July, and Optimedia assuring that their word was good and they don't "do" contracts, the team informed me that they would have to cancel the deal today. This, after passing on other opportunities with your competitors (because of the category exclusive we built in) and defending Denny's to other potential advertisers concerned that they would be in the same show as Denny's and that your brand wasn't "cool enough."

Money's tight, things have to be re-examined. I get that. I was and am really excited about Denny's and helping you re-vitalize your brand for this generation. My hope is that you can review what is below and either a) find 200K to do the deal internally or b) have some dynamite referrals to other CMO friends of yours that would want to buy against the 18-34 demo in Q1... I'm open for anything.

As I said - this is not a network backed show. I started the show when I was 15 on local access, moved it to Fox at age 18 and cleared ABC affiliates for my first season earlier this year at age 21. My business model is revolutionary for reaching TV and Gen Y viewers. This has been a dream of mine since I was a kid and the brand partners that are involved are a key part in defining this David and Goliath story. I created my show in a Denny's back in Auburn, Maine, and I have so much passion and excitement around the brand and what it can be.

I hope that you can find some way to help us out!
Thanks, Mark!

Cheers,
Jake

Imagine my surprise, when, during a holiday week, Mark called me.
"Jake, it's Mark Chmiel," the booming voice said.
"Mark, um, hi," I returned. "How are you?"
"I'm fine," he continued. "Listen, I don't have a lot of time and I don't really know who you are or what you do."
Shit, another pass.

"But from your email, you're one hell of an entrepreneur and visionary," Mark said. "I'll communicate the details with our agency, but your deal is back on. There's no way Denny's can afford not to support you. We'll find a way to make it work."

Euphoria.

"I...I...don't...um," I gasped. "I don't know what to say, Mark. Um, well..."

He completely knocked the wind out of me and he knew it. He was clearly in a rush.

"It's no problem at all. Just do what you do and we'll take care of the rest. Good luck."

And just like that, the deal, worth nearly a quarter of a million dollars, was back on.

Moments later, Nicole Ryan called.

"Jake, I don't know what you did, but Mark obviously really likes you. We'll send the paperwork right over for the deal and cut the check immediately. Congratulations."

"You mean, you're not...angry with me?"

"Why would I be angry?" Nicole asked.

Because I went over your head!

"You're a passionate guy and we see that. We just don't have the power that Mark has as the executive for Denny's."

And that was that.

Our Denny's partnership included a concert music series on *The Edge* as well as two 15-second commercials per show. We featured pop-star Andy Grammer just before he broke big, as well as nine other up-and-coming artists.

It just takes one YES.

Now I had two.

I took on the system and didn't make an enemy. I think it said more about Nicole and her ability as an ad executive to separate herself personally from the business she handled. I admired her.

I was rewarded for hustling and maintained a high level of integrity and trust with Nicole and her team, even though I had to go over her head to make it happen.

Don't kid yourself. People like Nicole Ryan at Optimedia are the exception. But they are around. If you are vulnerable enough to share who you are out loud, people like Nicole will show up and support you, even if it's uncomfortable for them.

I'm still friends with Nicole even though we haven't done business together since 2009. We talk several times a year and I like her very much.

Some people, like Nicole, will respect the hustle, others, like Coca-Cola execs, will be weary of it. Either way, it's none of your business how others think about you. Proceed boldly and without apology.

Many will not understand your boldness. But if you find a way to stick around in business, those who are apprehensive will eventually become allies.

They'll be enamored by your crazy ways and want to get closer to the flame. It's sexy to be mysterious. And if those who started out as skeptics never become enamored by you, then you probably never wanted to do business with them in the first place.

27

REMINDING YOURSELF OF YOUR GREATNESS

Why the hell can't I live in a free hotel suite for a year in San Francisco? Stranger things have happened...

We've switched from a culture that was interested in manufacturing, economics, politics - trying to play a serious part in the world - to a culture that's really entertainment-based.

— STEPHEN KING

I would've never thought I'd have been a millionaire two times over by the time I hit 25. Unfortunately, I hadn't learned how to keep it. That's okay. Because I've learned that if I do well enough each time I'm at bat, I'll always get a chance to come back. Striking out doesn't mean I can't play again.

I was having one of my classic downturns. I was financially dry for several months, not generating any revenue despite my best efforts. I never take my eye off the ball, but always use the quieter times in my career to reassess how I'm approaching my business and my life.

During a meditation while in New York City I realized that the muscle of doing business needs to be exercised, even if it's not for the TV show. If I can remind myself what it FEELS like to do a business deal, any business deal, then I could use that and replicate it again on larger deals.

With this acknowledged, I started daydreaming about what I could create that would be fun, and help me reinforce the idea of what it feels like to do a business deal.

The Edge had been back on the air for almost a year in syndication on CW and FOX affiliates nationwide in 35 million homes. Thanks to David Steinfeld, a syndication executive with over 22 years of experience at Viacom, MGM and *Saturday Night Live*, we cleared *The Edge* in such large markets such as Dallas, Houston Minneapolis and Seattle and mid-sized markets like Jacksonville, Milwaukee, Providence, Birmingham, and Austin.

It was a quiet yet focused return to TV in almost five dozen cities across the country. Steinfeld got me on the air and retained two-year agreements with the networks, all but guaranteeing me 100 weeks of airtime.

I was mainly on at midnight and 12:30a.m., going up against Craig Ferguson and Jimmy Fallon. I came in third in the ratings, but we were always pleased that in larger markets, *The Edge* did fairly well.

It was a dream come true for a kid who had struck out at bat a year before. My only responsibility was to continue feeding the networks with shows.

I ran out of money to produce new shows, though, and I was getting nervous about how many repeats of old episodes were beginning to air. Each week a repeat aired, I lost viewers. It was very frustrating to not be able to serve my audience with new programming, especially since they were so loyal to me, both on TV and on social media.

I needed to jump-start the deal making, but I wanted to do it in a non-traditional way. I wanted to live in San Francisco. I knew, intuitively, that if I could live there, even for a few months, that the energy in California would contribute to my clarity of mind and overall state of wellbeing.

But how do you move to San Francisco when you have an apartment in New York City and barely enough money to cover your rent?

Living in a hotel

I'd have to live for free without sleeping on someone's couch. Living in a hotel was the only thing I could think of.

I told a friend over coffee, "What if I can convince a hotel in San Francisco to give me a suite for free for an entire year?"

My friend laughed, but also knew that my wild antics often turned into an incredible windfall of surreal life events. The seed was planted.

I've always been curious about farming out the cost structures in my life and creating a "barter lifestyle." It had been working so far with Air Tran Airways, whose free, unlimited, first-class airline tickets anywhere in the world continued to afford me a lifestyle I had always dreamt of as a kid. Ford gave me a car. Kashi regularly sent palettes of food to my home and office. It was an experiment with brands taking care of the costs of my life that lasted for several years.

Idealistic and blissful.

I decided to go after it.

Jake gets Personality

I researched a bunch of boutique hotels and innovative entrepreneurs in San Francisco. I found Yvonne Delet-Lambert, President & Chief Executive Officer of Personality Hotels, who owned seven hotels in downtown San Francisco.

Every news article described Yvonne as an outrageous and smart entrepreneur, and one hell of a marketer who learned the hospitality trade from her father—a real estate mogul in San Francisco. Yvonne's family is the second largest owner of rental real estate property in the entire city of San Francisco, in addition to owning nearly a dozen boutique hotels in the area.

I decided Yvonne was the woman I needed to meet, and that I simply had to seal this offbeat deal with her.

I phoned the corporate headquarters in San Francisco and asked for Yvonne. I got the Marketing Director, Erin Finnegan.

Erin was the brain trust who helped to increase Personality Hotels bookings by making it culturally and socially relevant on Twitter and other social media. In fact, I learned that Twitter accounted for 20-30% of new bookings and new customer acquisitions for Yvonne's San Francisco hotel empire.

I pitched Erin my idea.

I live for free for one year, and I create a PR megastorm about the non-traditional approaches to marketing that Personality Hotels is pioneering.

Erin wasn't having any of it.

But I was determined. I checked out other hotels in San Francisco, yet something told me that if I could get Erin to buy in, that Yvonne would buy in as well. I called Erin back two weeks later.

"Erin, it's Jake," I said nicely.

Erin was playful in her frustration with me, having already told me no, but was kind enough to listen.

"Please just hear me out. You're all about personality and variety. The only way boutique hotels like yours are going to remain relevant are if you do off-the-wall marketing stunts."

I paused for a dial tone. Turns out Erin was still listening, so I continued.

"And you need to market to cities and people around the country who are coming to San Francisco, which is why your Twitter initiatives have been so popular."

I suggested by having a TV personality, who was also the youngest host in late night TV, living in her hotel for a year, that it would create a story that bloggers and magazines would want to cover. (To top of it off, the property that I was pitching to live in is called Hotel Diva, strangely aligned with my Diva-like approach to business and life.)

"So you want to live here, for free, for a year and your team is going to get people talking about that?" Erin inquired.

"Yes," I assured her. "The only cost to you is the cost of the room, and I'll even give you guys an out-clause after six months."

Erin asked a few other questions. Half-satisfied by my answers, she made an offer.

"You live in New York?" Erin asked.

"Yes but I'll come and see you anytime."

Calling my bluff, Erin offered a meeting with her and Yvonne, the CEO, the following week.

I quickly accepted. Erin was surprised, but intrigued.

I called my best friend Anthony David Adams, a genius in his own right, and told him to pack his bags for San Francisco.

The following week, Anthony and I were in a cab to the airport where we'd board our Air Tran flight, first class, to San Francisco. During the cab ride, I told Anthony that my plan was to live in the penthouse of this San Francisco hotel for a year in exchange for media attention and impressions. He loved the idea.

Anthony is one of the rarest folks in the world.

Currently, he's fulfilling a childhood fantasy by trading his way to space—literally. He started One Toy Spaceship and is trading with people for higher value items and, ultimately, for a ride to space. He also created Credit Covers (skins for your credit cards) and was the founding member of Summit Series, now one of the most prolific Generation Y leader youth summits in the world.

What I love about Anthony is his unmatched intellect and the way he literally can suspend reality and re-wire your mind in a single encounter. We've traveled around the country together frequently, often creating absurd and memorable moments (for ourselves and anyone daring enough to step into our path).

That's me and Anthony hanging out with our Air Tran friends on a layover in Milwaukee. We flew Air Tran almost every week in those days, so the staff got to know us on the plane and in Air Tran hubs like Atlanta, Milwaukee and Orlando.

Whether we are hijacking the Minneapolis St. Patrick's Day parade by riding in the convertible next to the "king and queen" or showing up and hosting a Google Island event off the coast of Sarasota, Florida, or riding mopeds in the Spanish Virgin Islands and getting arrested for speeding, Anthony and I have a history of disrupting the status quo, and often rejecting it all together.

We met when he was a guest on an earlier episode of *The Edge*. The appearance was a disaster, but somehow we remained friends. In the segment, my producers booked Anthony and his brother, Broadway star Nick Adams.

Nick Adams is currently starring in Bette Midler's *Priscilla* in New York and has been on Broadway for years. I didn't know Anthony or Nick, so I proposed an awkward segment including the three of us playing Twister with a local New York City prostitute. Naturally, the interview fell apart before it began.

Be careful what you wish for.

After the six-hour flight, Anthony and I jumped on the BART subway, and headed for Hotel Diva, located in the Union Square district of San Francisco.

I'm in the center, and Erin Finnegan of Personality Hotels is on my right. To my left, Julie, is a friend I made on a tiny Caribbean island. I brought Julie and Erin to a warehouse party when I was in San Francisco doing my deal with Hotel Diva. Always keep clients happy.

We arrived exactly at noon for our appointment with Erin and her boss, the CEO of the Personality Hotels, Yvonne Lembi-Detert.

"Jake, what do you want me to say I'm doing here with you?" Anthony asked, as we entered the hotel.

"Just make something up dude, whatever feels good," I said.

I threw caution to the wind.

Who cares what he says, just as long as he doesn't try to fuck anyone. (Anthony's been known to "date" several women at once).

I flew 3,000 miles cross-country with no money for a meeting with the CEO of a $100 million hotel chain in order to live there for a year, rent-free. This was all done on the off chance that they'd buy into the craziness and consider the proposal.

Erin, Personality Hotels' marketing diva, met us in the lobby. She oozed with sensuality not dissimilar to Marilyn Monroe. Her bleach-blonde hair draped her shoulders, parted perfectly, with bright red lipstick accenting her seductive lips. Her designer heals click-clacked as she made her way to the lobby.

This chick is completely Anthony's type.

Sure enough, Anthony clocked in. He was falling.

"Jake, so nice to meet you," Erin started out.

"Thank you for having us, Erin," I said. "Meet my friend Anthony."

An awkward hug between Anthony and Erin ensued, followed by giggles.

Erin led us to Yvonne's corner office.

Yvonne was sassy, brilliant, cunning with her remarks and sophisticatedly chic. She reminds me of a sexier Barbara Corcoran from *Shark Tank* on ABC. Yvonne and I connected immediately. Her energy and questions were relentless. She was curious about who in the hell I thought I was charging in her office proposing this deal.

And I shot back telling her she needed me if she wanted her hotel to be more innovative.

Erin became a distraction for Anthony. Both were leaving much to be desired. They looked like they were going to undress each other in the meeting.

"So, after six months, you'll move out if we don't like you anymore?" Yvonne asked bluntly, cutting into my insecurity.

"That's right," I said. "Think of it as an experiment. Let's outline a clear set of objectives and terms and then stick to it."

Yvonne had a reputation for being a risk-taker.

I'm addicted to both the art and science of a business deal. Psychologically, selling is a science. Creatively, coming to terms and packaging a compelling story, selling is an art.

Most of all, I loved being in the driver's seat, acting half the time as if I'm on a dare, sometimes turning a corner just to see where it lead.

Isn't this what life is about?

I need to know what it feels like to do business again.

"We'll think about it and let you know," Yvonne graciously said, ending the meeting.

By that point, Anthony had run off with Erin.

No surprise there.

As to whether or not their friendship was consummated, I believe they are still friendly to this day.

28

ACTING DECISIVELY

How a guy on a plane handed me $2,000 and why that taught me that "doing it" is always better than "thinking about doing it"

When I started out back in Louisville, there was Harry Collins. He was my first teacher. He saw that I was so obsessed with magic that he taught me the love of magic.

— MAGICIAN LANCE BURTON

A week later, Personality Hotels committed a suite for a year, with an option to exit the deal after six months.

I was elated.

You see what I just did there? I changed the game. By keeping it fresh, I kept my mind opened to new and almost unimaginable possibilities. By taking a sharp right turn, I was detaching from the challenges of my business, giving the challenges space to breath. Problems cannot be solved on the same frequency in which they were created.

Deliberate distraction can be your best friend when solving a problem in business. Don't take my word for it – try it yourself.

Yvonne and her team were spot on in their evaluation of our business deal—no stone left unturned and every question asked. In hindsight, the problem with this business transaction was me.

I was so eager to move to San Francisco that I overlooked all the details of our partnership. I promised that we would film TV integrations for my new show within three months, when in reality, it could take *much* longer. I also promised millions in PR impressions within six months.

While not outrageous deal points, I hadn't talked this over with my sales team or senior team and instead impulsively did the deal, chunking it up to figuring it out when we got there.

That's the difference between an exceptional business deal and another cautionary tale that ends up in a book like this. When you're writing your own rules, it can be difficult to see blind spots. The most important piece to any major deal is communication and clarity. The terms are secondary, although equally important. The clarity empowers your team, it empowers your partner and it manages expectations.

I used to think that big powered chief marketing officers would ignore me if I didn't flex my muscle and sell them the idea of pulling off amazing feats in record time.

Counter-intuitively, most marketers don't care. Time and time again, it's become clear that they care more about the quality and about their expectations being managed as opposed to delivering the *best* results or in the *quickest* time.

For years, I've built a brand on being the *fastest* and the *loudest*. I thought this was the best way to grab market share and get people's attention. I've realized that my most sustainable partnerships have been where I've properly managed expectations from the time I've pitched the business.

Yvonne faxed the contract to me. I signed and dated it and, just like that, I traded media PR impressions for living rent free in San Francisco for a year. Just like I had intended weeks before. I booked my Air Tran Airways flight to San Francisco. I planned to depart in two days.

My bank account tried to advise me otherwise. It was overdrawn by $157.23. Only one of my accounts was in good standing (with only $137 left). Ah, the irony.,

Screw it let's do it

As my roommate Mokay drove me to La Guardia Airport in Queens, we passed over the Triborough Bridge. The sun blinded us, which hid the tears that rolled down my cheek as I gazed toward the skyline.

New York City breathed such life into my dreams and gave me such a sense of self. It educated me, it exhausted me, it tore me a part and it built me back up. New York City has been my home and my place of work. It had been the city where I've had spiritual transformations and a city that has re-shaped what is possible in my life time and again.

Yet I was thrilled be to leaving. I was thrilled to move to a quieter part of the country with more peace than New York. The experiment of living in a hotel for a year was exactly what I needed. In my heart, I knew I'd be back in New York once I solidified a deal to produce new episodes of my TV show.

Fuck it, I shoot some episodes in New York, I fly back to live in San Francisco. I've got a free place to stay and free airline tickets. What's the big deal?

It felt good, and sounded even better, but life never ends up quite as you expect.

It's kind of like skydiving without a parachute.

You may think I'm crazy, and as I remember my emotions riding to the airport, I'd say it sounds crazier in hindsight than it felt that day. There is nothing more powerful for capacity building and becoming superhuman than pushing yourself to the point of no return, and having to see it through.

Whether going to San Francisco with no money, or running across the Brooklyn Bridge during a sudden torrential downpour, doing what you think is impossible is the best way to transform.

The thrill of the unknown far outweighed any damage it took to get there. I wasn't born this way – I studied people like Richard Branson, ballooning around the world to market his Virgin empire, or Steve Jobs getting fired from Apple (only to be re-hired and being responsible for saving the company). The rush of adventure and business thrilled them.

Some people do drugs to achieve that *alive* state, others have kids, and others have eccentric sex. This just happens to be the way that I feel alive – putting myself in nearly impossible scenarios and forcing myself toward solutions.

I sat down in my first class seat as the coach passengers made their way down the aisle.

I knew that I wouldn't have free first class airline tickets forever and I appreciated every single time I sat on an Air Tran flight.

Just then, The Question Mark Guy walked in.

Yes, *that* question mark guy. Matthew Lesko is the famous guy from the infomercials who screams at you about FREE MONEY from the government. I recognized him because of his bright blue suit, with yellow question marks hand-sewn all over it. To complete his ensemble, he donned a pair of bright orange glasses.

This is a publicity shot of Matthew Lesko, AKA the Question Mark Dude, who enjoyed coach on Air Tran.

I expected him to sit in the empty seat next to me. Instead, a broad-shouldered German-looking dude sat down. Matthew Lesko, FREE MONEY from the government info-product star, sat in coach.

Wait. What?

I couldn't believe that the self-made man who talks about getting FREE MONEY from the government for thirty-five years couldn't afford to sit up front.

After takeoff, I asked my flight attendant to deliver some first class snacks to Matthew Lesko in coach.

"And who shall I say it's from?" the flight attendant asked, smirking.

"Just tell him it's from TV's Jake Sasseville, and ask him how the view is from back there," I said.

I watched her deliver it to Matthew Lesko in the last row of coach. He chuckled, and instructed the flight attendant to give me his card and cell phone number. I continued sending him drinks and granola bars the whole flight.

Meeting a mentor

I found out the German-looking dude next to me was named Roger Scommegna. He appreciated the absurdity I was causing.

Some call it childish. I call it living in the moment. It seemed funny to send food back to a guy in coach that, if his branding were authentic, would be sitting in first class (there were two seats available).

I started talking to Roger. It turns out we had a lot in common.

Roger made a ton of money producing real estate infomercials in the 1980s (hence his interest in the Question Mark Dude, a fellow infomercial star). Each week, Roger's staff, from his hometown of Milwaukee, churned out over 200 individual infomercials featuring homes for sale in almost every major city in the United States.

By his mid-20s, he was generating $10 million a month—all achieved years before Internet marketing.

This guy is a genius.

"What business are you in now, Rog?" I asked.

"Three Thieves winery is one of the top in the world," Roger told me. "We sell wine in boxes."

Roger's spun his wine passion into a profitable business as well as TV series on food channels and commercial licensing deals.

I was deeply inspired by Roger. In many ways, he did with real estate what I did with late night television, with a twenty-year gap. (I was still in the womb in 1985 when Roger generated his first $10 million).

He produced on a national platform, but catered to a local audience. My "Jake after Jimmy" social media campaign was localized, but *The Edge* TV show was on a national platform. We were kindred spirits and we both knew it.

I was sad to depart, but I had a feeling we'd know each other for years to come.

I shook his hand and took his card once we landed.

"It was such a pleasure to meet you. I feel totally inspired" I smiled.

"It was a pleasure to meet you too," Roger said. "Call me anytime."

I arrived at the Hotel Diva armed with two suitcases ready to move into my new home.

This is un-fucking-believable.

Check in was a breeze and the Hotel Diva staff was alerted that their newest guest (and first ever full time resident) would be arriving. They showed me to my room and delivered a small fridge.

I didn't even unpack before having a *Home Alone* moment. I jumped on my bed with both televisions blasting music videos (I had two flat screens in a three-room suite).

I love this city and I feel so good here.

I'm sitting in the suite of my new home away from home, taken moments after my arrival. It's too Diva, even for me.

Over the next few days, I set up my ideal schedule. I meditated in the mornings, went out for walks all around the city (sometimes for two or three hours) then returned back to the Hotel for meetings and pitches. In the afternoons, I'd do more walking, have coffee with friends and end up at a garage party or art gallery in the evening.

This is the life.

I nourished my spirit and my soul. With all the soul searching (and finding), I grew weary of my financial situation. My bank account was nearly empty. I was spending extremely frugally, only $10 per day. I didn't know where I'd get more money. I had no credit cards, and though I was making progress with my sales, I hadn't closed a deal in a long time.

My free fall without a parachute continued to speed up. But the exhilaration remained. I had to figure this out because the ground was getting closer and closer.

There is a delicate balance between freefalling without a net and stupidity. Many people in my life found it hard to understand why I would put myself in this situation.

But the truth is, it's really not that bad. Again, I believe that no matter what, I'm always taken care of. That is my foundational belief system. From that place of certainty that I'm always okay no matter what, life becomes magical and stress-free. It's when I deviate from this place of certainty and start listening to the "noise" of "society" that life gets "stressful."

A mentality of lack as a child drips into adulthood

Growing up, my family didn't believe they were worthy of having a lot of money. My grandparents spoke poorly of people who had money, claiming they "think they are better than us."

From what I learned, I adopted a belief system of lack in my younger years. It justified poverty. The mindset didn't reward ingenuity, abundance or innovation. It pushed it further away. I've had to work through this limiting belief system in my adult years to get where I am now.

Part of the way I learn and grow is by scaring the shit out of myself with circumstances like my Hotel Diva San Francisco living experiment. At the time of this writing, I look back on these events (just two years ago) and I know I'd never put myself in a situation like that again. Lesson learned.

Back at Hotel Diva on a beautiful spring day in April, I sat on my couch and wrote out options to find a couple of thousand dollars to hold me over a few weeks. It had worked out nicely so far, but the reality is I have to eat.

One of the ideas that kept coming up again and again was to call Roger, the guy I met on the plane.

I didn't have any reason other than I felt intuitively he'd understand my situation and maybe he'd have the financial ability to help out.

Roger told me to call anytime.

Usually quick to act on my crazy ideas, I felt some resistance to call him.

Am I the type of person to meet someone on a plane and two weeks later hit them up for money?

I dialed his number in my iPhone and erased it several times before I finally chose to hit Send. My palms were sweaty.

"Rog, it's Jake," I said.

"Hey, Jake!"

"Are you in the Bay area still?"

"Hell yeah. I'm just up at my vineyard," Roger said, "What's up? How's life at the hotel?"

"Well, I'm in a situation and I need some help"

I took a breath.

"This is so odd for me to ask you this, because we just met and all, but I thought you'd really understand."

"What do you need?" Roger asked.

"Could I borrow some money for a few months?"

Roger thought for a moment. And by a moment, I mean two-seconds.

"Sure, how much you need?" Roger asked. "My tank is full and I'm happy to help if I can."

"Two grand," I said, feeling relief in my shoulders as I sighed.

"I'll pay it back immediately once I close a deal."

"No problem, I trust you Jake."

Roger offered to put the cash in my Bank of America account that afternoon.

I couldn't believe it. I thanked Roger profusely.

"No need to thank me, Jake. Everyone is a little broke."

Roger continued. "It's just money, its fuel for the tank. I'll fill you up."

And like that, the conversation ended.

The next morning, Roger's $2,000 was in my account.

I sat on my bed that morning, considering what had just happened. I closed my eyes and thought about how grateful I was, but how I didn't want to have to depend on people's generosity to fund my dreams or life-style. I craved stability, even though I knew stories like this would be great to tell years later.

I also considered Roger's approach to money: "Fuel for the tank of the car." I liked looking at it that way. It's essential for the car to run, but the fuel is not the car itself.

That changed the way I thought about my own financial state, where I wanted to take my business and how I want to treat others.

I'm forever grateful to Roger for these lessons. I paid him back within three months and we remain good friends to this day.

29

STAYING IN THE GAME NO MATTER WHAT

Life gets Xtreme: When you get lemons, make lemonade (with or without the pitcher)

All the evidence shows that God was actually quite a gambler, and the universe is a great casino, where dice are thrown, and roulette wheels spin on every occasion. Over a large number of bets, the odds even out and we can make predictions; that's why casino owners are so rich. But over a very small number of rolls of the dice, the uncertainty principle is very important.

— STEPHEN HAWKING

Only a week after Roger deposited $2,000 into my bank account, I received a call from the president's office of one of the largest ad agencies in the world, Alliance Agency, a division of Grey Worldwide Advertising. I met Amy Tunick years before when she was a senior development director. She's now the President of the agency.

"Jake here," I answered the phone, mouth full of pad kee mao from the Thai restaurant next door to the hotel.

"Jake," the woman said. "It's Jessica Weintraub from Alliance."

Jessica was Amy's second-in-command and a development director for the entertainment marketing agency.

"Amy Tunick gave me your name and number and suggested we speak about our new Pringles Xtreme brand launch," Jessica said.

I stopped eating and grabbed my notepad, chocking on the spice.

Jessica explained that Pringles Xtreme was re-launching in the 18-24 year old marketplace. They wanted to re-launch with me in the driver's seat. Ironically, even though I had been calling several dozen agencies and brands since I had arrived in San Francisco, I hadn't called Amy or even considered Pringles.

"Amy has asked that you be on the short list of people who we discuss this with," Jessica explained.

"We'd love to see what kind of ideas you have for Pringles Xtreme so we can present it to the client."

"Sure, Jess," I said enthusiastically. "How soon do you need something?"

"We're moving quickly on this. Can you get us something within the next forty-eight hours?"

A call out of the blue. And they want to move faster than I do.

"ABSOLUTELY."

It was Tuesday.

I called my business partners immediately. I briefed them on the opportunity and we put together three pages of ideas that afternoon. We submitted them to Alliance Agency and got swift feedback.

"Great work. The client likes all of it," Jessica told me a few days later. "They'd like to execute on a contract and a campaign."

I emailed Amy Tunick a private email letting her know how grateful I was that she believed in me, and thought about me five years after we first met.

I told Jess we'd send members of our team to her office to hash out the final details. I was still living in the Hotel Diva in San Francisco. I had to move decisively and without delay. Deals like this are fragile until they are signed, so you want your eye on the ball and nowhere else.

This was just the big break I was looking for.

After three weeks of negotiations and contracting, Pringles Xtreme bought integrations on my TV show, a digital campaign and a contest to be featured on both mediums. Still later, they threw us more business including PR events to support the partnership and then they bought title sponsorship to my Campus Music Tour that was kicking off in the Fall 2010 with J. Cole and We the Kings at 18 of the biggest campuses nationwide.

Did I have the know-how to pull this off?

Sort of.

Why did I take the deal?

For starters, it was a lot of money. Secondly, I had recently been reading about the life of Henry Ford. Ford didn't know how to build a car, but he knew how to create systems that would produce vehicles and he knew how to attract the best and brightest individuals who specialized in the areas he didn't.

Financially, the Pringles Xtreme deal netted my company its largest single payday ever. While I'm contractually not allowed to disclose the amount, the offer started out in the low six-figures and quickly rounded out at nearly seven figures.

Photo credit: Anya Garrett. This photo was snapped as my team placed a life-sized Pringles Xtreme hat on my head. They made the hat with Pringles cans for our photo shoot with Advertising Age. The article in AdAge talked about how we're changing the face of the entertainment and advertising industry. Pretty cool for a kid from Maine who's just wanted his own TV show since he was 15.

I can't help but think of this deal in comparison to the previous forty-five days leading up to it. From an overdrawn bank account, to the generosity of Roger seven days ago, I was flying high with a huge win with Pringles.

Like with all huge wins, if I had blinked or given up a day before, like so many people do, I would've never been able to take advantage of the Pringles Xtreme opportunity.

It's also fun to consider that Amy Tunick, president of Alliance, was not on my call list while I was in San Francisco. Sales and business, much like physics, is simple mathematics. What caused my deal with Amy Tunick and Pringles Xtreme to work was due to a simple equation:

Momentum = Mass x Velocity

When you have momentum, you are on the move and it will take quite a bit of effort to stop you. Your "mass" are your ideas, your brand, your past success and your team.

This is why so many people remain stuck.

Have you ever met someone who is extremely talented or genius-like, but they can't seem to get the momentum? It's because mass is not the only thing that matters in order to get momentum. Velocity is essential.

Velocity refers to the rate at which an object changes its position. It's the idea of how often can you try something and fall flat on your face in order to get the lessons and move onto bigger and better lessons. That's the trick.

If you move one step forward, and one step back, then you have no velocity. You create a lot of frenzy and energy, but you don't actually move beyond the point at which you started.

Are you seeing where I'm going?

Many people in my life, especially former business partners, have expressed how frustrating it is that I have so much energy and am constantly moving. I make a lot of mistakes, but I make more mistakes in a single 12-month period than most people do in a lifetime. The key is that even while I've taken two steps ahead, and sometimes fall three steps back, I always increase my movement forward, even if it's only by a step or two.

In sales, I have so much momentum that even though I can get 200 NOs, it only takes one YES. After every call, I analyze what worked and what didn't, and leverage those lessons in future calls. I maintain a high state of mind (by exercising frequently throughout the day, meditating, having coffee with friends) and remain focused on the idea (the mass).

In the end, your speed at any given moment doesn't matter as much. On a fifty-mile road trip, your speed might fluctuate from very slow to very fast. What's important is your *average* speed.

I shared my good news with Yvonne and the Hotel Diva staff and while they were sad to see me go, they knew I'd be back soon. I had the hotel staff pack up my room and put it in the basement. It was a unique relationship I had at Hotel Diva and it got me back on track.

30

THE FINAL IDEA

Why feeling good trumps everything – everytime.

If had a penny for every strange look I've gotten from strangers on the street I'd have about 10 to 15 dollars, which is a lot when you're dealing with pennies.

— ANDY SAMBERG

Do you want to be living a difficult reality that 99% of the world is living? Or do you want to be part of the 1%?

It's your choice.

I'm not talking about a Wall Street movement. I'm talking about a state of mind that enables you to do, have, be, desire, experience and achieve anything you can think or dream about.

Only in the last decade have I recognized the simplest secret of life. It is, indeed, a gem: to create magical results and get everything I want, my only obligation is that I must *feel good*.

That's it.

Feel good.

This whole book was meant to share with you that *choosing to feel good* is the most important choice you can make.

This boils down to two direct action items. The first is to feel good. The second is to recognize when you don't feel good, and find ways to feel better.

Nobody wants to be around someone who feels badly or even worse, someone who talks about feeling badly. Nothing is created from a place of lack or feeling bad.

What does emerge from feeling badly is clarity on what it is you want to be feeling instead. Focus on that. Reach for it.

For example:

> I am experience XYZ feeling. It feels shitty. This is causing me to *really want* to be experiencing ABC, which feels better just to think about.

> Focus on what it might be like to feel ABC. Drop all focus on XYZ, and only use it as clarity for what it is you *really want to be feeling* (ABC).

Getting sued by a former business partner? Don't like the feeling? Focus on what feels good. Even better, find something to *appreciate* about the person that's sueing you.

No money to go on a vacation? Find something in your reality that feels good right now – a great relationship, a beautiful home, a plant. And focus on it.

It feels good to feel good. And it's addictive. And it's sexy. And it's life-giving. And it feels good to feel good.

My dad has Parkinson's disease. Parkinson's is a chronic, progressive disease of the nervous system marked by tremor, muscular rigidity, and slow, imprecise movement, mainly affecting the elderly.

My dad was diagnosed when he was 40 (he's just turned 53). Even as the chronic condition makes his days more difficult, my dad teaches me more about feeling good, the importance of acceptance and about universal love than anyone else in my life.

He finds reasons to feel good, despite a reality that is challenging for him sometimes.

99% of humanity observes their <u>current reality</u> and *then* chooses how to feel based on the observed reality.

(Re-read the line above before moving on please.)

Observed reality: It's snowing outside.

Feeling: That sucks, I really wanted to go for a run outside.

Observed reality: That guy just screwed me over in a business deal.

Feeling: Fuck him, I'll sue him and get revenge.

Observed reality: They cancelled my flight and have poor customer service.

Feeling: Overwhelmed, frustration.

1% of humanity focuses on how they want to *feel first,* then they observe reality around them. By doing this, they create what the 99% call "magical" results. You must first <u>choose how you feel</u>, *then* observe your reality, not the other way around.

I know it's counterintuitive. Feeling good is a muscle that must be developed, but it's worth the time and energy if you want to achieve massively in any area of your life.

Plus, it'll make you a lot more fun, interesting and dynamic to be around. People won't know your secret – but they'll be curious as hell how you do it.

I'll admit it. When I'm bummed out I've been known to cry in the bathtub while listening to sad French music by Edith Piaf. Sometimes three baths a day.

But, as I allow myself to feel the sadness fully, I equally remind myself that when I'm ready to not feel this way any longer, that I can spin out of it when I choose. I give myself permission to feel how I feel and I release the resistance. The net result is that I achieve a higher level of spiritual awareness. Everytime. And I usually stay "somber" or "sad" for a fraction of the time as I used to.

This isn't self-help nonsense. This is how the laws of the universe work. Look no further than peak performance gurus like Warren Buffet, who cited

221

in an interview recently that "universal love" is the most important factor in his life and business. Steve Jobs was guided by Buddhism and was married by a Zen roshi. The most successful people in the universe understand the laws that are in play and are using them to their advantage.

Are you?

Even when I've had no money (or plenty of it) I'm proactively choosing how to feel, not allowing the money in my bank account dictate how I feel.

Focus on feeling good, THEN observe your reality. You won't be invincible, but you'll feel pretty damn good most of the time.

Death as an example of feeling good

Inevitably, folks ask me: "How can I feel good when the situation is bad?" People will give the example of death. How can people feel good when someone dies?

We experience death through the lens of how society tells us to experience it, instead of actually considering how we want to feel about it.

When my brother died, I was 17 years old. I was ashamed to express how I felt on that day.

The truth is, even though it was emotionally traumatizing, I felt relief for him, for my parents and for me.

Everyone else was sad. And they let me know it. After the wake, and a day before the funeral, my family and I went to a shopping mall and bought Hawaiian shirts.

Why?

It was my dad's idea.

It was time we led with a celebration.

We looked ridiculous showing up at Holy Cross Church in Lewiston, Maine on June 29, 2003 with our flamboyantly colored shirts, but it worked. My dad even wore orange pants.

The church was packed with men, women and children in dark colors. As we entered with our Hawaiian shirts, sorrow and grief quickly shifted to whispers and a buzz. Many smiled and a few laughed.

We chose to celebrate instead of mourn.

Being choosy

Every moment of every day, we choose how we want to feel. Be deliberate. Then see if you can maintain a baseline of feeling good *regardless* of what's happening during your day.

Even if the future seems dark and success impossible by everyone else's standards, you must decisively ignore the noise and choose to focus on what feels good.

For all the times I've let myself become part of the 99% and felt shitty based on a current or unwanted reality, the results have been equally shitty. Always.

If you've experienced any amount of success in your personal or professional life, you know one thing is for certain, even if you haven't acknowledged it – **you still want more.**

Always.

Esther and Jerry Hicks are authors of *Law of Attraction* and *The Astonishing Power of Your Emotions* among other best-selling titles. They liberated my attachment to my own desire for success with one single thought:

You'll never get it done and you can't ever get it wrong.

Focus on making one good decision at a time. You've experienced success, you'll want more. You'll never be done (except when you die). Failure is inevitable, welcome it in, fastly and furiously. And, my life continues to be a living, breathing example of how you can never get it wrong.

What an incredible experience to live your most authentic, good-feeling life. Subconsciously, by doing so, you'll be instructing others that they can feel safe to shine brightly, too.

The End... and the Beginning.

47158774R00149

Made in the USA
Middletown, DE
17 August 2017